Love

A User's Guide

KNOWLES, Jane. MB, BS MRCPsych, Mem. Instit. Group Analysis, is Consultant Psychotherapist to West Berkshire and an Associate of the Group Analytic Practice in London. She is also tutor to the Certificate in Psychotherapy awarded jointly by the Department of Psychiatry and Department of External Studies of Oxford University. In addition she is the Medical Director to the West Berkshire Priority Care Service NHS Trust.

Love
A User's Guide
INTIMACY FROM BIRTH TO DEATH

Jane Knowles

Pandora
An Imprint of HarperCollinsPublishers

Pandora
An Imprint of HarperCollins*Publishers*
77-85 Fulham Palace Road,
Hammersmith, London W6 8JB

Published by Pandora 1994
1 3 5 7 9 0 8 6 4 2

A catalogue record for this book
is available from the British Library

ISBN 0 04 440855 2

Typeset by Harpers Phototypesetters Limited,
Northampton, England

Printed in Great Britain by
HarperCollinsManufacturing Glasgow

Contents

Introduction:
The Facets of Love

Definitions of the word 'love' are many and various. Love can mean a warm affection, an attachment or fondness. It may relate to an object, a place, a person or an attribute of a person. It can suggest sexual passion or religious benevolence. We can feel it, send it to another, and fall in or out of it. It represents a part of our most intense emotional experience in relationships. Yet, when we say the word to someone else, can we ever really be sure of what we mean, or of what they will understand by it?

If we are lucky we are loved, albeit somewhat abstractly, from the moment our parents know we exist. The experience of being loved *in utero* has to be a speechless communication, a sense of intense belonging, of being contained somewhere safe and all-providing. Such a providential start to life becomes part of that person, built into the basic fabric of their personality, against which all other experiences will be measured and judged. However, for most of us, even at this very early stage of our experience, love is not so straightforward. Parents are very often ambivalent about a pregnancy; even a wanted child may cause anxieties and resentment from the beginning. Mothers' experiences of pregnancy differ both because the physical realities are widely various and because their internal emotional reactions are equally diverse. Thus the foetus *in utero*, whose understanding is limited, may experience these changes physically. The experience of being loved is built into the growing body. In some ways this causes many, if not most, humans to be searching constantly for that loving experience to be repeated throughout their lives. Too often the love we continue to seek as adults has not learnt the early lessons of love's imperfections, but maintains hopes of perfection. Perhaps each foetus needs to bear a little disappointment about the quality of its loving environment as preparation for life's realities. In each chapter of this book, I will explore a different aspect of the multifaceted experience that is love; the best and worst of our emotional ups and downs throughout life.

A mother's thoughts about her baby, her belief systems about what sort of baby she will have, and her anxieties about the physical development of the baby during pregnancy will all affect the way she will relate to her offspring. To a large extent that beloved foetus is a fantasy baby and many mothers continue to weave the fantasy through the early months or years of their child's life. It is hard to see your own infant clearly. Of course it seems to be the most beautiful, most perfect and most intelligent. Only very obvious 'faults' will make an impact on that maternal vision; in many ways the pain of giving birth to a handicapped child comes from the parents' sudden experience of the death of their beloved fantasy child to be replaced by the real one. For most parents, however, this is a prolonged experience, stretching over many years, as we gradually allow the misty illusions we create about our offspring to dissolve, revealing their true selves.

Early love experiences are often mirrored in our future love experiences. These, also, tend to have a rather vague focus on the realities of our loved one. We cannot see the faults and are dazzled by the positives. As time passes our understanding of our loved one becomes clearer. This process may mean a deepening of the feelings of love and attachment, a greater sense of true recognition of each other, or it can be a terrible disappointment, a process by which the loved person dissolves to be replaced by a reality which we could never have loved. The extent to which our parents love us, firstly without judgement or condition, and then gradually for who we really are, will make a major impact on how we feel about ourselves in love relationships and how accurately we see those we grow to love.

During the first year of life the baby experiences love being given to it and sucks in this experience as hungrily as it does food. Indeed babies who fail to thrive are as likely to be love deficient as food deficient. Babies who do not experience a loving environment seem to give up on fighting for life, and refuse food or become uninterested. The baby has a powerful need to be at the centre of its mother's attention, and most mothers find it impossible not to respond to this need with a form of maternal preoccupation, which can often exclude everyone but the baby.

As the baby develops the capacity to love, so the

parents learn how to be loving parents. Both are learning new forms of the love experience through the medium of their relationship. Throughout this book we will be looking at the emergence of love within relationships, parent/child, man/woman, man/man and woman/woman, as friends, lovers, children and parents, brothers and sisters.

Clearly, the early experience of love is different for first and then subsequent children. A second or third child never has the mother's absolute preoccupation that first children sometimes achieve. This may mean that a first child's expectations of 'true love' are different to those born later in the family. Subsequent children may represent a betrayal of the perfect love from mother for first children: sibling rivalry can be based on real hatred and rage. Such people may demand exaggerated commitment from future partners to stave off fears deriving from early experiences.

If those who are meant to love us instead threaten and abuse us, hurt and frighten us, then we grow to believe that these are the experiences of love, however distorted. We may not trust any further love which does not contain elements of abuse within it. What we experience when young is what we come to believe is normal: we can only compare it to other people's experiences much later in life.

During the child's second year there is a major developmental shift from being loved, being the centre of attention and being narcissistically interested in the self towards a recognition of others, and the building of a capacity to love in return. A child needs a sense of self-esteem to be able to love others as separate entities. The more he or she is able to bear the awareness of separation, and the greater autonomy involved with the physical changes of freedom of movement and control over bowels and bladder, the more he or she will become loving to others, people and things. Those who do not overcome this developmental hurdle remain self-preoccupied and unable to love others, while often still craving love and affection from them. Our capacity to love and have concern for others becomes an important motivating force in how we direct our lives. Those without that capacity have only their inner drives and desires to guide them; they may become anti-social, and in extreme cases perhaps psychopathic, as a result.

As the infant grows, so the circle of those who are loved grows too. From this more general love comes the ability to make friends, and to form loyalties to ideals as well as people. Once into adolescence, sexuality becomes an important aspect of love. The sexuality of earlier relationships is in the realms of fantasy, or should be in non-abusive families, but the teens bring the fantasy into reality. We have cultural expectations that love and sex are linked, religious teachings which declare that they must be linked, and social expectations that they should occur together. This is the romantic view of adult love which hopes that sexuality will be controlled by the force of love. Of course the real picture is more complex: love means different things to men and women throughout their development, a fact which we only slowly discover. Adolescent love can be both enthralling and disillusioning; sexuality can be a very much stronger drive than love, particularly in the teens and twenties, and excitement can seem much more important than security. The sense of love may still conjure up images of infantile dependence and relationships with parents that the growing person is trying to get away from.

There is also a strong degree of competition in love. Who you love and who loves you are important parameters by which people are judged, particularly in younger life. The choice of love object (person) may not be a straightforward emotional response, but a sophisticated social decision. It may be a matter of where you live, where you go to school/college, and where you socialize which sets limits on who is available for you to love or be loved by. Many people settle for loving someone because it is sociologically convenient. Research in America suggested that most people fall in love with someone who lives within three blocks of their own home! Some work hard at making others love them, but their goals are rarely just for love. Adult love and sexuality compound the many paradoxes and ambivalences of early love experiences, lifting adult love into an arena of such complexity that it defeats many.

As adult years pass by, what many experience as the intense need for sexual partners tends to become diluted by increasing need for a wider friendship network. While close familial love remains at the fulcrum of existence for many, ongoing 'friendship love' may be the emotional safety net into which we fall in order to share fun or grief. The benefits of the less intense bond which is friendship love often come in the form of flexibility and a greater degree of honesty.

In its intense form, love is almost always accompanied by hate. When it is experienced less intensely, the opposite side is also more dilute and more bearable. To a certain extent, we can write our own rules about what love within friendship consists of, whereas the rules of sexual adult love are written by society and they do not, by any means, suit everyone. Some of those rules suggest that adult love should have children as its direct public expression. It is still hard for couples to deviate from this norm, however much they may want to. And when we do have children, parenthood changes the pattern of our love relationships forever from a one-to-one relationship into triangular, square and ever more complex love formations.

Late middle age can be experienced as a time of returning to the opportunities for simple one-to-one love again, and yet this seems not to be the case for a large percentage of relationships. Couples lose each other somewhere in the three-part transition from couples to family to couple-with-grown-up-family. In addition, by middle age other loves – not only other people but occupations and hobbies – as well as friends and children compete for love. To juggle with these multitudinous loves, fulfilling responsibilities while meeting your own love needs is hard.

Some people generalize their capacity to love in relationships to objects, ideas, or activities. Others may replace the need to love people by these alternative investments of love. Extremes of such displacement might exclude commitment to a person, and commonly a workaholic adult puts responsibility, status, income in front of personal love. We all have to balance our love investment, but we each achieve a different and unique balance between people and objects, between practical caring and high ideals. The development of this balance, sometimes described by psychoanalysts as fundamentally different for men and women, will be explored.

For each blissful moment when new love is born and flourishes, there is an equal and opposite dark and tragic moment when love is lost or dies. This may be the falling-out-of-love experience when you wake one morning to find that you no longer feel the way you did; or it may be the death of a loved person. It may be betrayal at the hands of someone you continue to love, or the departure of a much-loved child who then never writes or visits. It might be the friend who moves to Australia or the parent with dementia who no longer recognizes you. Each of these experiences represents a loss, a blow to your love network, a sudden displacement of the balance of your love investment. Such losses constitute the greatest psychological stresses that most of us ever experience. They are the truly testing moments when we are aware of being sadly alone, inconsolable and bereft. Although we all know that time heals, these wounds often feel as if they can never heal. Even the healing leaves scars. Sometimes these scars can strengthen and finally enrich our understanding of love: a widower who was happily married may try to find new love; a couple who have grieved for their child may find courage to conceive again. Dealing with the loss of love, however it occurs, is as essential an ingredient of our lives as loving and being loved.

Many older people find that their love world contracts as friends and loved ones die and their own mobility and energy decreases. Others find that this is a time when they can rest happily in their relationships and experience them as more rewarding and less demanding than at any other time in life. Throughout life we need to be able to respect and care for ourselves if we are to be able to love others. If life experiences help us to come to accept ourselves as integrated humans with strengths and weaknesses, we are much more likely to be able to accept that our loved ones are also similarly flawed and that love is, in its own right, a flawed experience. That acceptance requires that we give up our hopes for perfect love − and our rage that we have to relinquish such an attractive fantasy as perfect love. The gain from this is a capacity to love which endures and nurtures us to the end.

Starting with an investigation into Greek mythology, this book intends to explore love in all its splendours and catastrophes, its beginnings and endings. It is an ever-present emotional dimension of life, and yet throughout each life it retains its mystery and unpredictability. We can never know what love has planned for us in the future, but in understanding our experiences of past and present love, we may hope to deal with the surprise a little better.

1

Greek Mythology

> Boy returns after heroic exploits,
> Boy meets girl and falls in love.
> There is a second suitor, but girl
> loves our hero more. After some
> arguing hour hero wins her hand
> in marriage. Then the troubles
> really start. . .

Modern day prince and princess? No. Well, yes, them too, but the story comes straight from the Greek myths. It may seem strange to start a book about love with a chapter on Greek mythology, the myths being noted as much for violence and retribution as for familial or passionate love. However, just about every great love story which as existed is recorded in the complex and ambiguous mythic form, so much truer to life than romantic fiction.

What myths make clear is that no one lives happily ever after. Love cannot exist in a vacuum kept preciously safe from all of our other emotions, but instead has to live alongside hate, greed, envy, jealousy, passion and revenge, as well as caring, nurturing and tolerance. The love we tend to focus on exists between two people, encapsulated and protected from other relationships, but more commonly love is found in triangular relationships or even more complicated social structures such as the family. Each new pair of lovers believe briefly that they have invented the state, before they slide down into the historical and sociocultural soup in which we all relate, rooted in our parents' and grandparents' experience, and acting as the trunk from which our children's relationships will branch.

The joy of myths is that they can inform us of an external history and of internal fantasy at the same time. They have been likened to dreams, except that they 'dream' for a whole society instead of just an individual and therefore expose some of our basic relationship templates. The Greek myths are a record of the social nature of man and woman kind. As social animals, humans are condemned to love: within its complex confines those of us who are lucky find our meaning. Like dreams, myths mix material, changing it by displacement (the emotions of one character may occur to another), by condensation (many separate experiences are condensed into one story), and by censorship, so that we do not become overwhelmed by the story we hear. In the face of our hopes the subsequent disillusionment can seem very cruel. On the other hand, the mythic mixture of reality and fantasy of the most intense of human experiences may allow us enough distance to hear and understand without being too hurt or anxious about the fate of our own loves in life.

There is a powerful need in any love story for a hero and a heroine who meet, fall in love, overcome obstacles and are then reunited. Most cultures throughout history have had a need to look for heroes, often aggressive warrior-men; heroes are never rated on their sensitivity but on their achievements in battle. The story of this form of hero is well told in the myth of Heracles.

Heracles

~

Zeus, the most powerful of the Gods, decided to conceive a son who would be heroic enough to protect both morals and gods. He chose the beautiful and virtuous Alcmene to be mother to his fantasy, and appears, in his own way, to have chosen her for love. Most of his mortal conquests were achieved through brute force, but for Alcmene he impersonates her husband, Amphitryon (who is away on heroic tasks to avenge Alcmene's dead brothers). His impersonation is clearly good enough to fool Alcmene, who is greatly stirred by his accounts of heroic activities on her behalf. Her passions aroused, they spend a blissful night together, a night which Zeus contrives to make the length of three nights, so complex is the task of conceiving a hero. His desire is so great that he 'unyokes' time, quenches the solar fires and asks the moon to go slowly rendering all mortals so sleepy that they are unaware of his amorous activity.

~

This appears to be an archetypal romantic situation, in which the lovers 'could have danced all night' in the blinding fury of their love. That they have hidden motives should not surprise or shock us. All lovers are eventually exposed as having hidden motives. He wants his perfect heroic son from his chosen woman, and she has her fantasy hero returned from deeds which avenge her brothers and liberate her from grief. There are many motives less pure than these to topple us into three days of love.

~

Alcmene was so fooled by Zeus' impersonation of her husband that when Amphitryon returned home victorious the following day she was not so eager to embrace the returning hero. She had already expressed all her passion and gratitude. Amphitryon noticed her reluctance and sought advice, whereupon he was told of Zeus' behaviour. Whatever he may have felt about the god's assault, he was too scared of divine retribution to return again to his wife's bed.

~

In tales of love, life is never fair. That Amphitryon has been brave and honourable counts less than the sheer power of Zeus to have what he wants. How many lovers in history have lost partners because they were unable to produce enough love-power to hold them against determined competition? What is the nature of this love, though, which can seduce by deceit or be frightened off by the power of a god? What kind of love did either man feel for Alcmene? And how innocent and unknowing is the beautiful Alcmene that she cannot tell the difference between god and man? Is she spared from responsibility because she has been deceived? In love, do we get deceived or deceive ourselves?

~

The cuckolded husband may have feared Zeus, but Hera, his wife was outraged when she heard of his actions. Unwisely, Zeus had been unable to resist the urge to boast of Heracles' conception: indeed Heracles means 'Glory to Hera', a tribute unlikely to find favour with the betrayed wife! Having extracted a complex promise from Zeus about the hour of birth of a son becoming 'High King', Hera manages to provoke labour in Queen Nicippe, two months early, while obstructing labour in Alcmene until after the required hour. Heracles is therefore born late into his destiny, already the object of much manipulation by the gods. One day later Alcmene gives birth to the twin of Heracles, conceived with Amphitryon and named Iphicles.

Poor Heracles: not only conceived to be a hero to fulfil his father's greatest dreams but born of a woman who has lost her eight brothers in battle, been deceived by Zeus and now gives birth, unexpectedly, to twins by different fathers. Perhaps it should not surprise us that Alcmene finds no pleasure in these births but rather fears that Hera's jealousy might destroy them all. In order to avoid this, she decides to sacrifice the baby Heracles by exposing him on a mountainside. However, the gods, in particular Athene, trick Hera into a walk along the same mountainside and have her suckle the abandoned infant, thereby making him a god. Myth has it that Heracles is so strong that Hera withdraws her breast in pain and a gush of milk arches into the sky to form the Milky Way.

Further trials await the young god. Now embedded into the complex world of stepfather and stepmother, as well as ambitious father and ambivalent mother, he is tested throughout infancy by one plot or another.

~

Although this is probably a fine upbringing for a hero, it must be a questionable one for a future lover, husband or father.

~

Thus he became the greatest of all heroes. In the course of his first marriage, however, he was destined to be driven mad by Hera, who was outraged by his excesses. As a result of this madness he kills his own sons and those of his twin brother. This leads him to undertake his famous twelve labours: great deeds through which he seeks forgiveness and further heroism.

He returns from his gallant deeds only to find that he has to fight the river-god, Achelous, for his next love, Deianeira. First the two men spar with words in front of Deianeira's father, attempting to prove themselves the best man with the best lineage. The fact that Deianeira has a clear preference for Heracles makes little difference to the men's desire to compete for her. Achelous can appear as a bull, a serpent or a bull-headed man, but even as a man the waters of the rivers constantly run from his beard (small wonder that Deianeira might prefer Heracles!).

However, he can claim that if Deianeira was to marry him she would be the bride of the father of all Greek water, as opposed to being the wife of a stranger if she marries Heracles. Meanwhile Heracles boasts that Deianeira will be able to claim Zeus, god of gods, for her father-in-law if she were to marry him. Given the complexities of Heracles' conception it is easy for Achelous to suggest that Heracles was either lying about his father's identity or that his mother was an adulteress. In this challenge Achelous was probably not the first male to call his rival a bastard.

Needless to say a fight then ensues, but when Heracles gains the advantage, Achelous turns into a snake. This is a form of cheating, and we immediately know who the 'good guy' is and who will eventually win. As Heracles attempts to strangle the serpent, Achelous turns into a bull and still our hero wins, breaking off a horn from the fallen bull to present to Deianeira's father as a wedding gift.

Such is Heracles' preoccupation with proving his own worth that he remains innocent of Deianeira's true father, never knowing that she too is the bastard child of a god, Dionysus.

~

This intense rivalry for the object of our love is not so unusual: we often think we love someone or something more when we need to succeed against another in order to gain it/her/him.

How often our determined pursuit of the object of our love renders us completely blind to that person and their backgrounds, only to have us complaining years later that we were fooled.

~

Deianeira may have been happier with the handsome Heracles than the wet-bearded Achelous, but she was an extremely unhappy wife as far as his famous infidelities were concerned. According to the myth many years later Heracles and Deianeira come to a river in flood where they meet the Centaur Nessus who offers to carry Deianeira safely across while Heracles swims. As soon as Heracles sets off into the river, Nessus attempts to abduct and then rape Deianeira. Heracles, the hero as ever, fells him with a single arrow, but as Nessus falls he instructs Deianeira to mix his semen and his blood into a paste with which to anoint Heracles, thereby rendering him faithful forever. Even in the heat of the moment Deianeira keeps her head, collects the ingredients and never mentions the power she has gained to Heracles.

How many partners might wish for momentary abduction if it could wield such future power over their loved ones. Deianeira's brief absence, with the help of a little magic, does make Heracles' love grow stronger.

The story of love between Heracles and Deianeira reveals some of the many blemishes which disfigure 'pure love', starting in their case from the moment of their conceptions. Heracles, the product of the desires of the most powerful of gods and a mother whom Zeus deceived; Deianeira, the product of a god's lust for her mother. Both children had powerful fathers of whom they saw nothing and suspicious stepfathers with whom they lived. Are the scripts for our own love stories written so early in life?

Most of us would wish to have been conceived as an act of love between a mother and father who wanted us and who we grew up to know. Many people find the idea of lust between their parents not simply unacceptable but totally unbelievable. And yet we become parents as a result of sexual activity, children clearly result from our libidinal, sexual instincts as much as from our loving, nurturing, caring ones.

From birth onwards we seek and need love in order to blossom into loving adults and yet our earliest origins are probably not rooted in 'pure love'. Rather, we start out life as the result of complex confusions of male/female relationships, power battles and sexual intrigues. Does the love we endlessly seek, as if it is something we have known and then lost, ever exist, except in our imagination? 'Is love a fiction, an illusion of a weak mind shrinking from reality and if so how and why should our minds ever have created the "idea" of love?' (I. D. Suthe, *The Origins of Love and Hate*).

Despite their beginnings, both Heracles and Deianeira do seek love with each other. Their passion may be fuelled by Heracles, apparent willingness to die in his fight for her. Such juxtapositioning of love and death is seen in many of the great love stories, and while modern-day heroes do not usually do battle with water-logged beastly rivals, they do often place themselves at physical risk in order to look appealingly masculine. Meanwhile, women work at attracting and choosing such heroes, who still have undeniable social charisma and power. Thus those who steal cars to drive them crazily are taking the unemployed path to social heroism and attraction, proof of their masculinity, those who climb mountains or descend deep caves, those who fight for their 'mother' country in the 'mother of all battles' and those who fight bulls or hunt are all following, however madly, in the footsteps of Heracles. The danger of these acts of proving masculinity is that they expose the would-be hero to events which may destroy either him or emotional aspects of him. Many heroes return too emotionally damaged from their exploits to ever enjoy the love relationships which they hoped would be their prize. Even Heracles has an episode of madness.

Oedipus

~

A tragic train of events leads Oedipus to slay his father and then marry Jocasta, his own mother.

Jocasta and Laius are so worried by their child-lessness that Laius seeks the opinion of the Oracle at Delphi on their problem. The Oracle informs him that what seems to be a problem is, in fact, a blessing. A child born to them would, she tells him, be a son who would first kill Laius and then marry his mother. So frightened is he by this pre-diction that Laius sends Jocasta off to live outside the city, where she broods and plots. One night she creeps back to Laius and persuades him, in a drunken state, to make love. Jocasta, it would seem, far from being put off by the Oracle's pre-diction, actually seeks it.

The child so conceived is snatched at birth by Laius, who pierces his tiny feet with a nail and orders that he is to be tied by this nail to a moun-tainside until he dies of exposure. The shepherd who receives these orders cannot bear to hurt the infant, now named Oedipus, meaning 'swollen foot', and takes him, instead, to another kingdom where he is adopted by the king and queen.

Eventually, as an adolescent, Oedipus comes to hear of the prediction of the Oracle, and believing it to relate to his adopted parents, travels away from their kingdom. On his journey he meets Laius, who is travelling his own kingdom in search of an answer to the riddle of the Sphinx. Something about Laius' high-handed attitude to a fellow traveller incenses Oedipus who, out of char-acter, raises his hand and slays him, without real-izing that it is his father he is killing.

When he reaches Thebes, Oedipus can answer
the riddle, causing the Sphinx to commit suicide
and thereby releasing the city from her evil hold.
The Queen, still grieving for her husband so myste-
riously killed by a stranger on the road, marries the
stranger who has saved the city. The Oracle's pre-
diction has come true.

~

In analytical terms, the Sphinx is another part of Jocasta:
she represents the seductress mother whose existence
first despatches her husband across their kingdom to seek
an answer to her riddle and then, the King having met
his death, lures her son back to her bed. Some writers
have queried the innocence of Oedipus and Jocasta to
their true relationship during their lengthy and pro-
ductive marriage in which they had four children. Even
when Jocasta realizes that Oedipus was the stranger who
killed Laius and the prediction is true, still she says
'Chance rules our lives and the future is unknown. Best
live as best we may. Nor need this mother-marrying
frighten you: many a man has dreamt as much. Such
things must be forgotten if life is to be endured.'
(Sophocles, *The Theban Plays*) Perhaps Jocasta might have
added that many mothers had dreamt as much too. The
narrow line between the passion of love parents and
children experience for each other and the acting out on
that love in sexuality is all too easily crossed, now as
then. Again, the intensity of their love means that death
and destruction are never far away. Jocasta commits
suicide when she realizes that Oedipus is on the point of

discovering the truth, Oedipus blinds himself, thereby becoming dependent on their children, who in a variety of ways come to horrible endings.

Many Greek myths revolve around the love, honour and duty between parents and children rather than within marriages, suggesting that it is in these blood relationships that love is experienced in its most intense form, both for better and worse. They also tell of children's split loyalties between warring parents.

~

Agamemnon grows up as a refugee in the Court of Oeneus, Deianeira's supposed father. In manhood, his wealth and kingdom are restored to him and he goes off to wage wars and avenge himself. First he kills the King of Pisa, Tantalus, and takes his widow, Clytaemnestra, as his bride-prize. From such uncomfortable and unloving beginnings come four children, a son Orestes and three daughters, Electra, Iphigeneia and Chrysothemis. Given that Agamemnon killed Tantalus and Clytaemnestra's first child 'at her breast' in his initial attack on the city, it is possible to imagine the kind of conflict of loyalties and love these children felt towards their parents, and that Clytaemnestra felt towards her new husband and their children.

Having fathered these children, Agamemnon's thirst for war is rekindled by the discovery that Paris has abducted Helen of Troy, and he departs to seek revenge. In order to honour the gods and ensure good weather for his initial journey he takes

his daughter, Iphigeneia, under the guise of finding
her a husband, and sacrifices her.

~

Such behaviour is hardly likely to have increased his
standing in the eyes of Clytaemnestra or eased the conflict of loves and loyalties felt by the remaining children.
Although highly dramatized in this version, such conflicts
of loyalties in love abound in reconstituted families of all
sorts. The fact that our love for people will bring us
into conflicts between those people is especially difficult
for the children of estranged couples to cope with.

The special nature of the love between parents and
children, with its implications of responsibility on the
parents' side and honour and duty on that of the child,
makes it a particularly difficult emotional arena in which
to deal with split loyalties. As children we are vulnerable
to the opinions of those closest to us. If such opinions are
at odds with each other and highly coloured by hostile
emotions, children can be left confused and anxious in
the middle of a warring couple. There is an imbalance of
power between parents and children, and often a further
imbalance between the powers of mothers and fathers.
Those in the less powerful positions will be able to
exercise less choice about the outcome of any argument
or split. Power can be exercised internally via the conduit
of emotional connection or externally by use of financial
and other material advantage. Children are vulnerable to
all forms of power manipulation. Meanwhile, parents
caught in the breakdown of their own relationship may
view the loyalty of the children as of extreme importance

to the ongoing stability of their own psychological world, thereby relegating their children's emotional needs to second place in their considerations. Commonly in Greek mythology, children seem to be regarded as property to be disposed of, often unpleasantly, as one or other parent sees fit. In any parental relationship breakdown there is the danger that we regress to such unenlightened attitudes towards our offspring.

~

Agamemnon is away for ten years during which time he acquires a new love, Cassandra, who bears him twin sons. Clytaemnestra also takes a new lover, Aegisthus, who is said to have approached her with love for her symbolized in his gifts but hatred in his heart for her family. Given the heat of her own feelings, surrounded by the heady mixture of Aegisthus' love/hate and a court made up of a family who had many reasons to hate Agamemnon, Clytaemnestra plans to murder her husband and his mistress when he returns. Meanwhile, her remaining children, shocked by her infidelity and murderous plans, make their own plans to escape and plan revenge.

Upon his return Agamemnon is killed by Clytaemnestra but avenged by his son Orestes, who, supported by his daughter Electra, kills Clytaemnestra and her lover.

~

The children of this sad split family appear to feel that

the only way they can express love and loyalty to one parent is to murder the other. In the intensity of a Greek drama these murders are real. In the heat of modern divorce children feel that their love of one or other parent can still tear them apart until they have, in their minds, 'killed' the love and goodness in the other. Most researchers agree that the children who survive divorce best are those who can maintain realistic contact with both parents, thereby keeping both 'alive' in their developing emotional world. In the heat of a relationship breaking down it is often difficult to maintain this dual contact. Honour, duty and pride are all emotions that we commonly experience alongside love within family relationships. All too often the actions which lead from these feelings produce drama rather than security.

It is possible when reading the Greek myths to come to the point of wondering why the characters bother to love, have children or make wars, all of which seem irretrievably and unhappily linked. The underlying point seems to be that love, whatever its origins, mother/child, child/parent, partner/lover, cannot save us from our destiny or the ultimate finality of death. Indeed love is often linked with death and made the more poignant by this attachment. Byron said that 'sooner or later love is his own anger'. As many a tragic couple in literature, screen and stage will attest, we can love and value something or someone we are on the point of losing with a particular intensity. In that sense there is no salvation involved, although we may momentarily invest in it as though there were. In the first moments of love, be it in the arms of a lover or holding a new baby, it is possible to believe that time will stand still for us. Of course it cannot, and yet few of us escape life without having invested at least once in the magical time-stopping qualities of love. Those, for instance, who seek to cure the midlife crisis of 'discovering' mortality by falling in love again, often with someone many years younger than themselves, have discovered just how powerful the illusion of love's capacity to hold death at bay can be.

However, without love, even at its most distorted or hateful, there is also no relationship and no sense in human existence at all. For most of us it is the sense of importance we give to our relationships with others which gives life its colour and depth. The capacity to love and be loved is central to human experience. Thus with each opportunity we invest afresh in its unique charms to inspire, uplift and heal. We commit ourselves to moving mountains in the momentary certainty that anything is possible. It allows us to feel both strong and weak, enriched and eradicated, pained in our pleasure. The Greek myths give us an insight into the power of love which, in every generation and every culture, has to do battle with the other human powers of hate and destruction.

Every night we are all witness to the news from around the world which often portrays a world in which the darker powers appear to be winning. However violent the Greek myths may seem, human nature has changed little, and violence, within families and between nations, continues. Murder, rape, torture and pillage remain firmly in fashion whatever else may change. In the safety and security of our homes it is hard to be in touch with those dark feelings inside of ourselves, and yet we watch with a voyeur's interest to see just how bad human beings can be.

If we were without love it would be hard to find life bearable in a world where such behaviour exists. Freud talked of equal and opposite life and death wishes in the basic constitution of us all. These forces battle continuously inside ourselves. We work hard for success, and yet undermine ourselves too; we act out our loving, libidinal instincts alongside our instincts for aggression. The same man that will love and comfort his mother, feel passionately about his wife, and conceive and care for his child, will also take up a gun or a bomb to kill or maim another. It is the fact that these two are the same person which makes the behaviour so frightening, so inexplicable – and so human. The friendly neighbour who helps you for years can also find it in his heart to rape you. Similarly the murderer can also cry, the torturer fear pain, and the one who pulls the trigger feel instant regret.

Sometimes the dark side can masquerade as love, of person or place, as the excuse for the action. Perhaps this is the cruellest deceit of all. But the actions eventually betray the masquerade. The basic goodness of love shines as a hopeful beacon in our troubled world just as it did many many years ago in Greece. The Greek myths stand as reminders to us all that love exists within the context of wickedness, evil, tyranny and the misuse of power. Love creates its own special place in human nature wherein we can preserve the good, foster and encourage it in ourselves and others.

2

Developing the Capacity for Love

Birth and the Mirror-Image

A newborn baby is only aware of him or herself. Those aspects of the mother which he or she needs to survive, the food and the love, are viewed as aspects of the baby rather than part of someone else. In the turbulent world of a baby's emotions his or her needs are experienced intensely, and when the needs are satisfied the baby feels happy: when the needs are frustrated the baby experiences rage. Because the baby is only aware of the self all these emotions are experienced within that self-arena. So the baby is either satisfied with or furious with him or herself.

Parents who have a child because they need the child to love them often find these early days of infancy threatening and depressing. The baby's intense self-interest, to the exclusion of all other stimuli, leaves the parents with the sense of being unloved, often a familiar and painful experience. In the six or so weeks that it takes for a baby to become sociable enough to smile they may feel victim to the intensity of the baby's emotions. Survival needs dictate that infants have to be self-orientated. This is where we all begin the long developmental process which will finally enable us to be loving and caring.

Within a few weeks, as the baby's eyesight gains focus, he or she can see the mother's face. This is the first experience of the outside world and the baby views the face as a mirror reflecting the baby back to him or herself. Thus if the mother is smiling the baby will smile. As they smile together the baby experiences pleasure which encompasses both mother and child. The baby will intuitively be part of the mother's emotional world much as she will be a part of the baby's. If the mother is happy and relaxed the baby will assume those feelings too. If the mother is tense or anxious the baby will pick up those feelings.

At this stage the baby still assumes that the mother-mirror is a part of the self; if the baby feels safe with that assumed part of the self, it will be used as a receptacle for those emotions which the baby cannot safely contain within its own psyche. This process is called projection. If the baby feels unbearable anxiety this will be projected into the mother's emotions. An intuitive mother responds to this by reassuring the baby, thereby easing both the baby's anxiety and the anxiety she has felt as a reaction to the baby's projection. A parent who does not understand this process may instead feel acutely anxious without knowing why.

~

Trish had never considered herself an anxious person until she had Jamie, her first child. When Jamie was three weeks old Trish tried to take him for a walk but had to race home having felt overwhelmed by anxiety just fifty feet from home. As the weeks passed she limited her trips into the outside world in order to avoid the painful feelings of anxiety, but this avoidance imposed real limits on what had previously been a busy and fulfilling life. It was her mother who first suggested to her that some of the anxiety Trish was experiencing might be Jamie's. Just the suggestion was enough to make her curious about, rather than frightened of, the experience, and she experimented with trips out of the house on her own. To her great relief she found that she was not anxious except when with Jamie. She began to see that some of her emotions were directly connected to Jamie's new experiences of life and that anxiety was foremost among these. Discovering that she had the capacity to comfort and reassure Jamie left her feeling more capable, and less anxious too.

~

Part of the baby's anxiety will arise from the fact that the same mother who reassures and nurtures also sometimes frustrates and is absent. There is intense pleasure and intense rage in relationship to the same object. This is unbearable for the baby and so a split develops. There is perceived to be a good mother who pleases and a bad mother who frustrates. The good mother can be enjoyed and the bad mother attacked in the baby's fantasy world. Mothers who feel secure about themselves recognize these two powerful projections as originating from the baby. Mothers with less self-esteem or understanding of a baby's emotions may experience the projections as if they were real adult judgements rather than the baby's fantasies. Thus mothers can come to feel that they are either very good or very bad, or, more confusingly, both alternately.

~

Pamela and Henry were both determined to get parenting 'right' for their new baby, Astral. Both had read books and discussed infant care from the beginning of Pamela's pregnancy, and they therefore expected to be able to cope well in the first months of Astral's life. Sometimes Pamela felt as if she was living up to their expectations. Everything went smoothly, Astral fed, smiled, slept, and Henry was delighted. But two or three times a week Astral would scream and rage, be difficult to placate and make Pamela feel like the biggest failure in the world. Henry saw these times as 'getting it wrong' and became increasingly critical of Pamela, making her self-esteem plummet further. Astral picked up her mother's discomfort and became even more difficult to calm and so a vicious circle was established. In retrospect Pamela described it as being on an emotional switchback. Luckily a health visitor was able to help her establish a routine in which Astral was sometimes allowed to be grumpy and difficult and in which Henry's less than supportive comments could be dismissed.

Separation

As the baby's awareness continues to expand he or she begins to guess that mother is a separate being, a discovery which increases his or her anxiety. Knowing that mother is separate also means knowing how dependent on that other person the baby is. At the same time the baby begins to see that there is only one mother who is both good and bad. The mother who provides pleasure and is depended on is one and the same with the mother who frustrates, provoking fury and fantasized attack. Now the baby has a new anxiety, namely that the fantasized attacks will have hurt the good, needed mother. The baby's sense of omnipotence leads it to magnify the possible damage his or her fantasies are capable of. The baby feels the first stirrings of guilt and wants to make reparation in his or her relationship with the mother.

In adult relationships we often find remnants of this developmental process. Having felt angry and even destructive towards someone we love, it is easy to feel overwhelmed by guilt at the damage we have done. Conversely we may limit the amount to which we feel free to express justifiable rage with loved ones because our fantasies of the potential damage we may do are still as omnipotent as the baby's. Not all is fantasy, of course. The majority of crimes of violence take place within the home and within the context of love relationships: husband to wife, son to parents, daughter to mother. The hate which is the other side of the coin to love can sometimes rage out of control. Statistically however, murderous violence occurs in a very small proportion of love relationships, even though all of us have probably fantasized about it at some point, if only as an infant. The fantasy may act as an 'escape valve' for intense emotions, protecting most of us from actually murdering those we love.

This form of murderous violence is different, psychologically, from the more common versions of domestic violence, in that all human beings have the potential for experiencing murderous hatred as a basic building block in their psychological development. The controls on the expression of these feelings are also, for most people, a very fundamental part of their psychological make-up, which would only become disinhibited under extreme conditions such as social chaos or great provocation. Most domestic violence is connected to power and domination coupled with frustration in an adult setting, often precipitated by disinhibition caused by alcohol or drugs, and occurring in those who have witnessed violence between parents during their childhood. Such violence springs from later stages in our development process and may be connected to the individual's experience of sexuality.

~

Jane and Tony came for marital counselling when Jane became frightened by Tony's insistence that she was having an affair. No amount of reassurance would comfort him and he would follow her to work and regularly threaten to kill her when he discovered who her new sexual partner was. During this process Jane had come to feel frustrated by the irrational attitudes Tony expressed and agreed that she felt so angry that she might have to leave. It became obvious during the course of their assessment for counselling that Jane was assuming that the anger she felt which might lead her to abandon the relationship was of a similar intensity to that Tony was experiencing when he threatened to kill her. The counsellor explained to this couple that Tony's anger was of the sort which reflects an early, very primitive part of our development and the fact that no amount of evidence could convince him of Jane's innocence meant that the inhibitions against acting on primitive impulses were not fully functioning for him. In the calm of the counselling session Tony could state that he did not want to kill Jane but had been frightened that he might lose control on several occasions. This was news to Jane who said 'I had not realized the difference between being wildly angry with someone and the feeling that you might kill them.'

The couple separated for six months whilst Tony worked with the counsellor on his early experiences of abandonment, aged five months, in a children's home. Meanwhile Jane was reassured that this frightening experience was not, in any way, her fault and helped to see just how much Tony had forced her into the position of his abandoning mother, without that being her basic wish at all .

∼

We discover that many other aspects of love which we experience as adults are remnants of the child's early experiences. We certainly split off good and bad aspects of the personality of someone we love, heightening our awareness of the good and denying the bad to a considerable extent. During the course of a lengthy relationship we have to come to terms with those split-off aspects that we tried not to see. Many relationships collapse during this phase of discovering the reality. We also experience a sense of dependence on those we love which may or may not feel comfortable depending on our earlier experiences of dependence.

~

Lisa was born prematurely and her mother, who was diabetic, was seriously ill for some months after the birth. The family had many troubles throughout Lisa's childhood, which meant that she never had attention paid to her needs, but was, instead, expected to meet the needs of others in the household. During these formative years Lisa learnt to encase her needs within herself, denying she had them and becoming highly competent in meeting the needs of others. She became a nurse, and therefore went from her family into another institution which expected her to be a need-meeter rather than a needy person. Having never had a happy experience of being safely dependent on another, falling in love was a scary business, in which Lisa employed many tactics to keep Phil at bay. She was sure that he would reject her if he guessed how needy she was, felt that she too might be overwhelmed by her needs and feared that she might lose her job if she 'cracked' her perfectly competent caring facade. She also became depressed as she started to trust in the consistency of his care and attention to her, as this experience painfully underlined what had been missing in her early childhood.

~

Mobility

Mobility brings with it a new sense of autonomy for the baby. He or she is more free to explore now and is fully aware of being separate physically from the mother and others in the home. There is also a growing sense of being psychologically separate, of the inner world belonging to the self. Mothers can often sense when the baby has taken ownership of their psychological boundaries, experiencing a form of psychic separation from the infant's emotions. Mother and infant can now differentiate more clearly which feelings belong to whom.

By now the baby will have formed an opinion on how loved and wanted he or she is. They do not experience this as a thought but rather as a major building block to their developing psyche. Because their omnipotence still leads them to think that they are the centre of the world, many of the feelings around them which are not directly attributable to them will be included in their picture of their lovability. Thus if their mother is depressed they will assume that she is unhappy because of them. If she is frustrated it must be their fault. If there is tension and violence in the home they are somehow responsible. There is a limit to how much responsibility each baby is able or willing to bear however, and some will chose to feel no responsibility either because of their own limits or because too much anxiety is created in them by the emotional climate at home. Others will feel that they have to mop up all the responsibility for everyone's emotions. These basic patterns of relating to the feelings of others can get stuck for the growing child so that they will assume a similar position of responsibility or lack of it in adult close relationships.

One of the most difficult negotiations in many adult love relationships is a recognition of how limited is our power over – and thus responsibility for – the feelings of others. Of course we can avoid doing and saying the things that would be blatantly and damagingly hurtful (although as such things are said and done, most commonly, in the heat of the moment, even our control over these is limited). Happiness is an elusive feeling which we cannot necessarily produce in ourselves and certainly cannot be responsible for maintaining in others. We cannot control the flow of emotions between other family members either, although not uncommonly one family member, the mother or a child, is held responsible by the whole family for its communications and arguments.

~

With four teenage children, Jeanette assumed it was normal to feel exhausted emotionally. A college friend who had not seen her for many years visited and was appalled at the way Jeanette looked and felt. On being questioned Jeanette agreed that she took all responsibility for communications about everyone's activities and expectations within the household. She also wanted everyone to be happy, within themselves and between each other, and so used much energy each week explaining one to the other. Bob, the husband and father, was a peripheral figure who took no responsibility for feelings or communications within the family. Jeanette had set herself a task which no human could hope to achieve and which had little positive feedback for herself. Meanwhile the family had happily let her assume this central role because it protected each of them from having to assume responsibility for their own happiness and relationships within the family.

~

The narcissism of early life becomes converted into self-esteem and concern for others during this phase of development. The infant discovers the outside world and becomes less interested in the sensations from its own body. He or she can now delay gratification of their wishes for longer and longer periods of time if distracted by external amusements and adventures. For those who fail to make this developmental change their interests will remain primarily with themselves, their own emotions and their own bodies. This will always limit their capacity to form loving relationships with others, their love remains predominantly turned inwards to themselves. As we can only experience self-esteem in a relationship with others, most narcissistic people have little or no self-esteem, despite seeing themselves as the most important focus for the world.

The terrible twos

Towards the end of the second year, bowel and bladder control are achieved for many and this increases the sense of autonomy and powerful control. However, in the course of achieving this control they have begun to realize that they must conform to certain expectations of them and their behaviour if the love which was previously given unconditionally is to continue. There follows a time of revolution – often named 'the terrible twos' because it occurs between the ages of two and three – in which they fight to be allowed to get away with whatever they want to do, to dominate all around and to have their own way. In this behaviour they are searching for the boundaries to which they can go without losing parental affection. A world without boundaries would be a frightening place, however, so at the same time as trying to push their parent, they are also desperate to be assured that some boundaries exist.

We continue to push boundaries in any new relationship throughout life, to test out what we will be permitted to do before love or caring is withdrawn. Such testing behaviour is, however, greatly modified by our early experiences in childhood. If we have learnt to combine self-respect with respect for the boundaries of others, our testing of those boundaries will be a controlled and non-intrusive exploration of the values and expectations around us. If we have had little or no experience of boundaries as a child we may become angry when we meet adult boundaries, we may feel that rules are for others but do not apply to ourselves, and, in extreme cases, we may not even notice as we trample over the boundaries which are the rules and expectations of others and of society. Conversely, some children brought up in chaos create a safe psychological space for themselves by developing strict internal boundaries which make it impossible for them to test others out at all. Such people appear rather 'frozen' in relationships and often appear to be tolerating behaviour which others would find unacceptable from those closest to them.

~

As the child of harshly judgemental and physically punitive parents Jo had 'walled herself in' psychologically and determined to keep a safe space around her in any relationship. Because she was so passive within relationships both friends and lovers soon found themselves taking her for granted and even abusing her. This often made people back away but she met Bernade at a party and he fell in love with her passivity, believing that this was everything he had ever sought in a 'perfect' woman. Within the psychological walls Jo had established as a child she convinced herself that she was safe, even though Bernade was as violent and hostile as either of her parents had ever been. Increasingly unhappy, Jo sought help from a women's refuge. Alongside the caring and protection she received here, she also was encouraged to go to self-assertion and self-defence classes. The caring allowed her 'inner walls' to melt a little, backed up by an increasing sense of being able to protect herself better in the external world.

~

If parents are consistent but firm then healthy boundaries become built into the child's psyche, so that by the time they go to school they are capable of socially acceptable behaviour without much external adult containment. They develop a super-ego, an internal policing system, which tells them what is or is not right in relationship to others. They also use their parents as models for correct behaviour, wanting to identify with them and with the family standards as a whole. Obviously, if the family is disordered in some way then the child will incorporate that disorder into their understanding of themselves and the world.

Gender

Many of the differences between men and women in relationships arise because of the different ways in which parents treat male and female offspring, consciously and unconsciously. At birth often the first question the midwife is asked is the sex of the child. From that moment the parents and the rest of the family start making assumptions about that baby based on his or her sex rather than his or her personality.

The parents' own experience of being either male or female will colour their reception of the child. A mother who has been abused may receive a boy with a sense of revulsion and a daughter with foreboding. A father with a patriarchal background may welcome a son and heir and dismiss the arrival of a daughter as second-rate. Women are often said to be disappointed by the birth of a daughter. These reactions will all modify the love and care that the baby receives. The baby will perceive ambivalence, even dislike or disgust, when it gazes into the mirror of its mother's face — rather than unconditional love. The fact that parental opinion and approval often matters to people well into middle age should underline just how important it is to the infant and child, who knows nothing else by which to judge itself.

~

Trudy had been aware, from before beginning the pregnancy, that her husband, Ray, and his parents expected and wanted a boy. In all their eager discussions and preparation for the baby, it was always referred to as 'he', the baby clothes were knitted in blue and Ray painted the nursery blue even in the face of Trudy's uncertainties. When she queried 'What if it's a girl . . .' she was told not to be silly. In the first few days after Daniel's birth she felt as if she had been silly, and was greatly relieved to have pleased Ray so much. This happiness began to fade rapidly and by the time Daniel was six weeks old, Trudy had become depressed and unable to care for him. He was welcomed into his paternal grandparents' home and they took over the parenting for several months, during which, far from getting better, Trudy became increasingly guilty and despairing about herself as a mother, woman or person.

Increasingly left alone by the family, Trudy finally attempted suicide while on a psychiatric ward. Luckily the staff, sensing her despair, quickly noticed she was missing from the ward and found her with the bottle of paracetamol in the woods, in time to save her life. It was clear that this had been a serious attempt to take her life. When this was explained to Ray he pronounced her mad, unfit to mother and started divorce and custody proceedings. This final cruelty seemed to jerk Trudy back to life, and within weeks she had begun to fight for the custody of Daniel. She recognized that by giving birth to a son she had 'produced' a baby for 'them', which did not feel like her baby at all. This had made it hard for her to bond with him. The reality of the paternal family actively trying to remove Daniel from her custody for ever turned fantasy into real life, and enabled her to fight, and eventually win back, her rights to have the space to love her son freely.

～

Research shows that even in homes happy to welcome daughters there is a tendency for them to be breastfed for less time than sons, to be stimulated less, and for them to cause parents less anxiety. Mothers are described as having a 'push–pull' relationship with daughters, because they assume that they will grow up to fulfil caretaking roles and must therefore learn early not to be too needy themselves. At the same time, however, they know that there are still strong social limitations on what is allowed for women, and they pull their daughters into these boundaries tightly.

Sons are seen as rightly needy and dependent. For a woman who experiences herself as dependent on a man (and most mothers still do have this experience when babies are young) there is a comfort in having a little man in the household who is dependent totally on her. There is a common view that men remain children at heart, and therefore there will be much less pressure on the son to inhabit strict behavioural boundaries and more encouragement for him to have stimulation and adventures.

Even in households which actively try to prevent such stereotypical reactions, the gut feelings and experiences of parents and grandparents can easily surface and influence the emotional climate around the child.

The mother can also feel a form of passion for her son which will not be aroused by her daughter. Although this difference is not, by any means, universally true, many mothers will admit to a more passionate form of bonding with infant sons. If her sexuality is orientated towards males, her love for her son and daughter may reflect that orientation in their different qualities. A daughter may grow up wondering what is lacking in her that she cannot arouse that passion. Even adults become anxious and uncertain if they are posed questions about why it is less comfortable for women to breastfeed their daughters than their sons, for instance. Of course, the little girl can make little or no sense of the situation except to imagine that either something is wrong with herself as a child, or her mother as a mother.

While a daughter may yearn to get into a more passionate form of bonding with mother, a son may feel that he has to fight extraordinarily hard to get out of such intense loving. Particularly as he begins to seek autonomy he may feel that he has to forcibly push mother away, setting a future pattern of pushing away those women with whom he is physically intimate as an adult. This pattern of a woman trying to get herself into a position of being loved while a man tries to hold it somewhat at bay is an often repeated adult experience of the remnants of these early days.

Daughters who move from mother towards father in hope of more intense loving in the early years of life (before two years) may then sexualize their infantile needs for closeness and security. They may spend their adult lifetimes searching for male love to replace some quality which they perceived as missing in the original love from mother. As Clare, survivor of four marriages said to me, 'It has taken me thirty years of adult life to finally accept that my husband is not and cannot be my fantasized ideal mother.'

Men often describe a fear of losing themselves in close relationships with women, a fear which probably has its origins in their early struggles to escape from the intensity of mother's love. Such fears are normally in conflict with their equal and opposite need for intimacy and love from a woman.

Nigel, depressed by the breakdown of his second marriage, sought therapy to understand why he felt such strongly contradictory feelings in his relationships with women. He described a need to 'make them fall in love and be dependent' by trying hard to fulfil their needs. As soon as he had achieved this position in the relationship, twice within weeks of marriage, he felt an equally powerful need to push them away by hurting and humiliating them. He recounted an intense attachment to his own mother, who was alone with him for the first three years of his life because his father worked abroad. When the father returned he remembered a sense of fierce competition with him, followed by fear that his father would win through his capacity to make his son feel small and humiliated. In order to resolve this painful triangle, Nigel had pushed away both his love for and his identification with his mother. These feelings and experiences were now seen as 'cissy' and behind him for ever.

In adult life Nigel did yearn to recreate the initial intimacy he had known with mother, but as soon as this was achieved his young fears also returned with devastating results for his adult life.

~

Sexuality

In the pre-school years, the child will develop a sense of sexuality. In its infantile form this sexuality consists of an eagerness to explore his or her own body and, sometimes, masturbate. It is discovered to be pleasurable to achieve physical stimulation combined with fantasies of sexual relationships with the parent of the opposite sex. Children become competitive with the parent of the same sex for the attentions of the other. Some even fantasize about removing or killing the same-sex parent in order to possess the opposite-sex parent. Such fantasies, while exciting, also arouse guilt and anxiety. Eventually the guilt and anxiety become the predominant feelings and sexuality becomes submerged again until the body ripens in adolescence and makes them ready for sexual relationships outside of the immediate family.

Dealing with a child's early sexuality often causes anxiety for parents. It is hard to hit a balance between wishing to repress on the one hand, thereby avoiding any untoward sexuality between parents and child, and wishing to collude with the child's fantasies on the other, with all the inherent dangers of real adult sexuality and the sexual needs of the parent intruding on the fantasy-world of the child's development. This is a crucial phase in developing a sense of sexuality which is internalized as a complete part of ourselves, rather than as something we add on, with make-up or aftershave, in later years. If a child experiences a force to repress all such feelings and associate them with guilt, badness or sinfulness, their sexual feelings in adulthood will be contaminated by these early childhood memories. Many a lover knows how all-pervasive such inner messages can be, whatever the adult desires.

Kenneth and Mary came to the psychosexual clinic because both felt their relationship was strained by Mary's inability to enjoy sexual intimacy. Mary said that intellectually she would very much like to be able to relax and become aroused, but that she could only allow herself to go so far and then it was as if 'an electric switch was thrown and turned her off'. She described intense feelings of self-hatred at such moments, sometimes combined with rage towards Kenneth. Kenneth felt confused and hurt by this reaction. Although aware that her experiences were damaging to a relationship she otherwise valued, she also felt that maybe she was a 'good woman' because of her inhibitions. She said that these feelings came from an identification with her mother who had always explicitly stated that sex was 'for men' and revolting; something women tolerated with difficulty. Mary found arousal a frightening experience because it meant separating herself from her mother's experience. Such changes between generations in their sexual understandings have given rise to many confusions and much sexual angst. The internalized sexual being of our early childhood may be cruelly out of date with society by the time we reach our twenties or thirties.

~

Even more damaging to the developing psyche and the child's sense of sexuality is a parent who, for their own sexual needs, colludes with the fantasy of infantile sexual love or forces a child into adult sexual behaviour. Such experiences are often experienced by the child as 'fracturing' their development so that aspects of their personalities become shut off. More attention will be given to sexual development in chapter 5 on sexual elements of love.

When the child goes to school he or she discovers the fun of making relationships with friends and teachers. They begin to use all that they have learnt so far about love and concern of others and start to see how others perceive them. Families often distort what is reflected back to the child about his or her appearance, intelligence, lovability, making it greater or lesser than external judgements will validate. School and friendships are the natural arenas in which the child can, for the first time, begin to get a different perspective on the self and how it is received by others. This new experience will alter to some extent the original sense of self-esteem established in earlier years. Relationships outside the family are discovered to be less stable than those within, and the child may experience betrayal, teasing, abandonment and being left out, along with the rosier moments of friendship. His or her self-esteem needs to have been well established in order to survive these experiences without too much damage being done.

Sadly, many children's self-esteem is not high, and it is often these children who attract more than their fair share of victimization in school. Also, not all children have experienced stable relationships at home prior to school. One or both parents may have already been lost to the child, he or she may have experienced or at least watched violence and abuse in their closest relationships. These are the templates they then carry with them out into the world. Their expectations of all relationships are coloured by their early life.

School and its associated achievements and judgements make a big impact on our self-esteem and on how lovable we feel. However, if self-esteem starts high it will survive the knocks of failure, and if it starts low there will not be an achievement great enough to lift it. The child may struggle against its internal judgements on the self by trying extra hard to achieve, or may totally believe the distorted judgements of low self-esteem and give up with little fight. This sophistication of our self-esteem in relationships external to our families is important in how we relate to all new contacts, including those we will come to love, in adult life. To a great extent, people get accepted or rejected on the basis of how they 'carry' their allotment of self-esteem. Too little or too much will almost always invite rejection, or limited acceptance from others who also under- or over-value themselves. Thus the development of our self-esteem comes to play a crucial part in how we select future partners. The notion that someone 'is not good enough' for another is often used in connection with choosing life partners. We have to know about our own goodness and its limits before we can hope to make a happy choice.

Adolescence

In adolescence, sexuality resurfaces to change the face of relationships with both sexes. One sex now becomes the object of our passion and the other the object of our competition. Both passion and competition are heady ingredients and lead to an intensifying of emotional experiences within relationships. This is the stage at which hearts can be made to leap, and also, be broken. Experiences of pride and shame become associated with patterns of relationships. Although there is much investment of energy in relationships there is also little security in them at this stage. The adolescent feels little sense of security about their vision of themselves either, one day feeling wanted, loved and good about life, the next feeling unlovable and bad. Aggression and temper which they learnt to control in the terrible twos may resurface alongside their libido, making them feel totally out of control of their physical or mental internal worlds. The struggle to regain and keep control and achieve a stable sense of self takes the best part of ten years for most people.

Romeo and Juliet, probably the best-known adolescent love story, demonstrates the intensity of feeling which can ignore all other consideration, even survival. Many far-reaching decisions and actions take place in these turbulent years when, psychologically, we are not necessarily well placed to make them. Often it is during adolescence that we become aware of the extent of our intellectual development, although it may be many years before we know whether our education has been a good match for that development or not.

Intellectually we learn by two methods, originally described by Jean Piaget (1896–1980) a child psychologist. First, we assimilate knowledge by a process of intellectual absorption of things around us. Second, we learn by accommodation to new experiences, stresses and challenges. The first allows us a concrete view of the world and knowledge, while the second offers us the opportunity for more lateral and abstract thought. The way in which these developments are fostered and encouraged in childhood has an impact on how we perceive ourselves and others. Education can expand or limit our future choice of partners and our capacity to love and think about our love experiences.

And so we enter adulthood, and, usually, feel grown up. Only years later do we understand how naive about ourselves, others and relationships we still are at twenty, and what a lot we still have to learn! According to Erik Erikson, the first man to train as a Montessori teacher, at twenty we have only, at best, completed five of the eight developmental phases of life. He describes life stages in terms of what we need to achieve, or, if development is hindered, its opposite. Each of these stages has profound effects on our developing capacity to love ourselves and others. From birth to one year he describes a phase in which we develop trust or mistrust. From one to three, as we become autonomous, we can either enjoy that autonomy or become loaded with doubt and shame. We develop either initiative or guilt from three to six, and industry or inferiority between six and twelve. During adolescence we either establish our identity or suffer role confusion.

In early adulthood we chose between a pathway of intimacy with others or isolation with ourselves. Clearly the choice between these two pathways is greatly influenced by all that has gone before, although a life experience, particularly a traumatic one, can have long-lasting effects at this time. Intimacy naturally leads on to generativity, the desire to create either children, or works of art, important scientific contributions, something special which we can feel is uniquely ours but has to then stand in relationship to others. The opposite of generativity is personal stagnation. Finally, as we enter an aged maturity, the end point of all of our development will become apparent. Either we will have achieved a form of integrity which continues to allow us to relate lovingly to others, thereby mitigating the anxieties associated with personal mortality, or the approaching end will fill us with despair. All of these developmental steps take a number of years, even decades, and they are constructed one on top of the other as a lifetime of development. And all of this is based on our capacity to develop and sustain loving relationships.

3

Maternal and Paternal Love

Parental love is a complex mixture of instinct, learnt behaviour, duty and responsibility. It can be the most unconditional or the most demanding of loves, the most practical or the most passionate. Most parents find that their children can evoke feelings, both loving and hating, more powerfully than anyone else in their lives, a surprising discovery for many new parents. Children who are long since adults can also find that the feelings they hold for their parents still dominate their emotional life.

Maternal and paternal instincts are those behaviours which a mother or father, or someone in the role of 'mother' or 'father' performs without conscious thought. These may seem like rational, thought-out behaviours, but they arise in our minds at a level before conscious thought. These 'gut response' behaviours include a fierce desire to protect, to respond to, to control, to nurture and to help grow. Not all of them would necessarily appear very loving on the surface.

It is interesting, for instance, that most parents' response to a child who is in danger is to slap first and think later. Many then regret that slap in the heat of the moment, wishing that they could have dealt with the situation in a more considered and rational way. Yet the slap seems to come out of the parenting instinct as much as a desire to nurture does. Is this just because most parents were themselves slapped as children? Or is there an instinctual response to the child who seems to be in danger? A recent survey in Nottingham suggests that at least 65 per cent of mothers had slapped their child by the age of one, and that 95 per cent had slapped before the child was three. Although we are questioning whether or not slapping should constitute abuse and therefore be made illegal, it would seem that our unconscious parental behaviour still weighs heavily in favour of physical control and punishment. Many parents find that loving their children makes it very difficult to caution, restrict or punish them in an age-appropriate manner.

Learning to parent

Where do we acquire our parenting behaviour? Much of the way we find ourselves behaving as parents does not fit in with our considered academic notions of what is right or wrong. The reality of parenting is almost at odds with fantasy.

~

Kenneth wanted his family to be a relaxed and easy place to grow up, very different to the tense and frightened household in which he had been reared. Although they had discussed this many times, and his own wishes were shared by his partner, Angela, this couple still found themselves repeating patterns from Kenneth's early childhood. His tolerance for the behaviour of his two sons, aged four and one, was not high. Much as he wanted to laugh and play with them, he discovered that he was much more likely to be controlling their behaviour, wanting them to be clean and tidy, not wishing to be 'shown up' by them and, as he came to realize, deeply envious of their lives. Kenneth and Angela had four sessions of family therapy in an attempt to understand how they might appropriately control two boisterous infants while also feeling freer to enjoy their children more. Enjoying more of their time together meant that Kenneth could feel less envious of his sons. This enabled him to give to them emotionally in the way that he had previously only intellectualized about.

~

For better or for worse, much of the behaviour we will demonstrate as parents to our children will have been experienced by ourselves as children. Because our relationships with children tend to be on a more 'gut' level than our relationships with most adults, we respond to them with less thought and more instinct. Thus we are likely to repeat our own past experiences. Knowing this, some parents make conscious efforts to control aspects of their 'gut' feelings. By no means every parent who has known violence and abuse as a child will behave that way with their own children. However, they will probably have to exert more self-control in order to avoid it than parents who have never had abusive childhood experiences.

Fiona came into therapy when she discovered that she was expecting twins. She had made the decision to try and conceive only after years of thought and anguish, because she feared that her own experience of childhood would be repeated with her children. Her partner Barry had been patient with these fears, although he could not understand them, having no experience of childhood abuse himself.

Throughout her infancy, Fiona was left in the care of her stepfather while her mother worked nightshifts as a nurse. From the age of four her stepfather had come into her bedroom regularly and, with increasing intensity, abused her, finally having intercourse with Fiona when she was eight. The abuse continued until Fiona was thirteen when she told her mother. At first, meeting disbelief, Fiona felt even more isolated and unloved than before. Her stepfather turned his sexual attentions to her younger sister and attempted to silence Fiona with physical and emotional threats. Eventually the resulting tension in the house was so great that the mother was alerted to the problem and started to believe the daughters. The stepfather ran off, never to be seen again, and the mother struggled to bring about some reconciliation of all the family, while making it clear to Fiona that she blamed her for all their problems, emotional and financial.

Fiona remembers this stage of her adolescence as a time of fury at the world and everyone in it, but also as a time of being intensely shy among her peer group and embarrassed by her under-achievement at school. She recalls, with guilt, her wish that her stepfather, with whom she still believed she had something 'special', would return to make everyone happy again. In the face of the cruel reality of her experience so far, Fiona concocted a fantasy family in which she had lived where people were close and loving.

When Fiona was eighteen her mother committed suicide, the younger children went into care, and Fiona was launched into the world to start her adult life, with no qualifications and no means of support. The death of her real family meant that Fiona could invest even more in her fantasy world, in which she now produced a family story that replaced her own past. Any unwanted memories were split off and put away deep in her unconscious mind. This defence enabled her to work, study and eventually train as a nurse. In her fantasy world her mother had been a caring and successful nurse who combined work and family life in magical bliss. Fiona decided to follow in these footsteps. Barry and Fiona met just after she had qualified and moved to Sheffield to work. He was impressed by her dedication to work and her determination to be a 'healer' in many senses. As they started to fall in love he noticed that she sometimes seemed vague and preoccupied, and she noticed that she often felt anxious when Barry tried to kiss her. Suddenly she became aware of the past being stirred up like a sleeping dragon by her new-found closeness with Barry. Part of her wanted to run away but another part, yearning for love and intimacy, wanted to stay. This second part won; she did stay, and initially she attempted to live out the 'happy family' fantasy. Gradually, as present reality, the ups and downs of their shared life, was allowed to play an ever greater part in her vision of life, she shared the truth about her past with herself and then with Barry. By doing so, however, she became alarmed at the terrible gulf between her real life, both past and present, and her fantasy.

She knew that she had to be able to bridge that gulf by understanding her feelings about her abusive childhood and her ongoing search for the perfect family, before she could ever hope to cope with the psychological demands of mothering. In therapy Fiona relived with her female therapist many of the ambivalent and highly-charged emotions she had felt for her mother. She recalled the intensity with which she had yearned for her mother's attention and love, and how she had, at first, turned willingly to her stepfather's abuse believing it to represent the love she wanted. She often experienced the therapist as 'self-indulgent', 'self-obsessed' and also 'seductive': all ways in which she had, as a child, seen her parents.

But the therapist maintained a calm, warm and consistent persona in the face of Fiona's attacks so that Fiona could feel appreciated and 'held' emotionally while she continued her troubled explorations of the past. Talking through and emotionally re-experiencing in therapy helped Fiona to begin to understand her need of a perfect fantasy family: even now as an adult in a caring relationship she felt frightened and defeated by the weight of the abuse she had suffered. As a child it had clearly been unbearable for her to see her life clearly. By the time the twins were born, Fiona felt more at ease with herself. Despite this, there were still some hard times, particularly with the male twin, Jonathan, who could easily come to represent the unacceptable parts of herself for Fiona. However, knowing that she could take the worrying experiences of mothering to therapy helped her to cope with the memories and emotions which the twins' life evoked for her. Her relationship with Barry is stable and supportive and both feel, now that the twins are five, they have found a way through to realistic parenting, despite Fiona's tragic childhood.

~

It is difficult to know whether any of our parenting behaviour now comes from an inherited instinct before childhood experience is written on to it. The fact that some parents do have insight into their own potential weaknesses and care enough to change and control themselves would suggest that the strength of parental love makes it possible to overcome past disasters. Each generation seems to start off wanting to be better parents than their parents were to them. This means that we now set high standards of parental behaviour, which society monitors, and this can seem daunting to new parents uncertain of how their love will translate into practical reality. Whether our desire to improve parental standards with each generation comes from our love of our offspring or our competitiveness with our parents is a matter of opinion. By the same token there are undoubtedly some parents who had good enough parenting themselves but who find it impossible to be loving parents, because of their personalities or socioeconomic and educational restrictions.

The fantasy child

Some individuals and couples feel the pull to conceive a child as an emotional tug which arises out of their love for another adult, others as a pull towards creating someone to love them. Some think of the separate child they will produce, already loving the fantasy of that child before conception, others think of the child more as a lovable aspect of themselves. Whatever the motivating force, a child will have been loved and/or hated prior to birth. Few parents remain neutral until they get to meet the product of their conception. These emotions arise in the parents' relationship with their fantasy of this child, without knowing anything of its sex, its colouring, its temperament, its intelligence or whether or not it is handicapped in any way. Foetuses are experienced as perfect, as characters, even as evil tumours in their parents' internal world, without reference to who or what they really are.

This lays the template for many, if not all, of our future relationships having elements of fantasy about them. The people we love are not exactly as we would describe them but rather composed, in our minds, of aspects of themselves which we choose to see and aspects of ourselves which we project into a vision of them.

Once the child is born, parents have to come to know the real child. Sometimes this is a relief, sometimes a disappointment. The parents' capacity to love the child will reflect this early experience of relating to the fantasy child, which will be a reflection of the parents' early experiences and present needs. Many children spend a lifetime trying to make their parents love them more, without ever understanding that their parents' capacity for love in those earliest days of their relationship depended much more on the parents' internal relationship with the fantasy child than on the real baby, the real person that they were and are. Often this mode of relating, be it loving or hating, gets stuck for all the participants, needing an emotional earthquake, a sudden trauma, or a new family member to shift views later on.

~

Pauline was labelled 'a mistake' before birth: even though she was a good, perhaps abnormally quiet, baby, both parents experienced her and described her to each other as demanding and exhausting. As she grew older, Pauline realized that the family image of her was negative, and she tried hard to make little or no demands on anyone and to be as helpful as she could. All her efforts failed. The family had a fantasy of her which was impervious to new experiences with her, and so whatever happened it was their vision of Pauline that was seen and remembered in family mythology. It was not until Pauline was in a relationship during her thirties and her partner commented, with some irritation, that Pauline's total lack of self-assertiveness made him feel uncomfortable that she had a lightning bolt of insight. Suddenly, as if her own family mythology fell away like scales from her eyes, she saw clearly that far from being a demanding human being she was the reverse. Her family, far from meeting her needs and exhausting themselves, were completely unaware that she had any needs.

Pauline took a few months to come to terms with this new vision of herself. Much of the chronic sense of failure and misery which had pervaded her life seemed to lift with this more positive recognition of herself. Seeing herself differently meant that she commanded different feedback from friends, most of whom were only too willing to corroborate her new self-esteem. When she went home for Christmas it was with a sense of foreboding. The family did not spot the change immediately, but the way Pauline interacted with them, and in particular with her mother, was different and caused ripples of discontent in all the other family members. Before going home, Pauline had taken the chance to read several books on family dynamics and could therefore see how much she had been used by the family in the past. This helped her to stand up to their attempts to put her back into the scapegoat position.

A few days after Christmas her father phoned Pauline to say that her mother had become depressed as a result of Pauline's visit. This felt like an enforced rerun of much of her earlier experiences of her parents, but she was able to suggest that her mother's depression was not her fault or responsibility and that perhaps her father and the marital relationship was more to blame for much of their disappointment than she had ever been. Violent arguments erupted in the family with her brother and sister becoming involved with their parents in heated marital discord. Pauline could see more and more clearly that her role in the family was to act as the person blamed for everything so that everyone else could feel comfortable and happy together. As soon as she shed this role, each member of the family had to face their own disillusionments separately and with each other in new ways.

~

Family mythology about each of its members is a strong network of ideas which each person reinforces by the roles they accept and play. Many families find a scapegoat in one child, so that the parents and remaining children can feel happier and more secure in their relationships by comparison. Such roles may last for life if the scapegoat child is never offered the opportunity to reassess their position away from family pressures. Many adults feel pressurized back into their original roles as soon as they are in contact with their families. Parents, too, may act to reinstate the status quo whenever they are with their adult children, making it hard for these children to develop different aspects of their personalities. Clearly these roles either encourage the child, allowing their capacity of loving and being loved to flourish, or they can restrict it, even deaden it. In later life new experiences may allow the child to break old boundaries, and as in Pauline's case undo damage within the context of an adult relationship which was loving and encouraging. Sadly, many pick future partners who 'fit' psychologically into their distorted visions of themselves and who continue to limit or deaden that individual's original capacity for love.

~

From her earliest memories, Hanny's mother told her that she was a 'bad girl'. As she grew and entered school, Hanny was confused. Part of her believed that she was bad and that she would be punished, but part of her understood instinctively that her mother needed her to be bad and that was what would get her attention, albeit unpleasant attention. So she started to be difficult, to fight with other children, to fail at school work and to provoke teachers. Superficially she was punished for all these activities, but deep down she heard the satisfaction in her mother's voice as she regaled the neighbours with Hanny's latest exploits. Hanny's mother had been brought up in a strict home in which, particularly from the daughters, extremely good behaviour was always demanded. Her own naughtiness had been squashed but not entirely extinguished. Instead it lingered looking for a safe new home. The arrival of Hanny, her first daughter, gave her the opportunity to project all the bad she had had to contain into another, leaving her feeling good and pure again.

~

Many mothers experience a fierce surge of competition with their new born daughters, and an associated need to diminish their appeal to fathers and the rest of the family by projecting bad aspects of character entirely into them. Often this mode of mother/daughter relating lasts until the mother dies, and the daughter is still left feeling tainted and unrecognized however hard she has tried to make amends.

Mother and baby

Many mothers experience a preoccupation with the baby quite unlike any other feeling which relationships have stirred up in them previously. Love is a major part of that preoccupation, but anxiety also plays a large role. Although the baby achieves physical separation of a sort at birth, the mother and baby stay part of a closely communicating emotional 'one' for months. Thus the mother's self-esteem and feeling of well-being about herself and the baby will be experienced by the baby as belonging to her or himself. Similarly, the wide range of intense emotional experiences of early infanthood are often experienced by the mother as if they were her own. Thus maternal love at this stage is one of the many components of a form of emotional soup in which both mother and baby are submerged.

Mothers often question their love for the baby, or their capacity to nurture him or her at this stage, not because they are truly failing, as they fear, but because they are so awash with the baby's feelings as well as their own. Maternal love requires an emotional containment of the baby's intense emotions, allowing the baby a sense of security in the mother's indestructibility. This containment is hard work emotionally, and mothers who have low self-esteem or poor realization of psychological boundaries between themselves and others often suffer great guilt as they sink under the weight of the baby's frustrations, fury and attack. Rather than seeing that maternal love requires the ability to withstand this assault, they fear that it is in some way justified, that the baby is passing judgement on them and have failed to love sufficiently.

Father and baby

Paternal love seems to be expressed differently to maternal love. Much of this may be rooted in tradition, and nowadays couples may make conscious choices about how much maternal or paternal love each will demonstrate. However, the growing infant does need both forms of love from one or other parent.

The role of paternal love is firstly to protect the mother/baby duo from the external world. Thus his love will be demonstrated in practical ways that are necessary to achieve the protective role. For many couples with a first baby it comes as a shock to realize that maternal and paternal love are expressed in such different ways. Of course the mother can sometimes provide elements of the maternal, but many couples find that although they plan to blur or merge roles in advance, their 'gut' reactions to the baby are different from the beginning. For instance, while mothers tend naturally to wish to hold their infants in a firm and reassuring way, fathers often find themselves wanting to interact in a more boisterous and exciting way, even with small babies. It can be hard for both sides of the couple to feel positive about their partner's different interactive style.

~

Ruth found it almost unbearable to watch Bobbie throw their three month old son around as if he were a rugby ball! Meanwhile, Bobbie felt that Ruth was already being over-protective with his son, and worried about the long-term consequences. Arguments which could have lasted throughout their joint parenting began to sound increasingly bitter. However, Ruth's father pointed out that this was not an uncommon split between mother and father, because mothering and fathering was, and was meant to be, a different experience both for the adults and the child. He suggested that Ruth tried one throw of the baby to test out whether it was as dangerous in reality as she feared it was. Meanwhile Bobbie phoned his mother to elicit details of his early mothering. 'She says she spoilt me, and I'm alright,' he then announced.

This early experience of having to recognize each other as parents in their own right and developing trust in each other's different styles was helpful in many a potential argument in the future.

~

Part of the learning experiences of early parenthood is the vast array of different ways of expressing love for your infant. The experience of the emotion of love can also vary from a warm attachment to a fierce, almost burning adoration. As in all relationships, love matures. As the parents get to know their baby and value aspects of his or her personality, so their love becomes more focused and less generalized.

Parenting and envy

The capacity to give love unconditionally to infants is not inherent to everyone. It is a draining experience, even to those who have themselves been much loved. For those from less stable backgrounds, they are loving out of an emotional overdraft. The adults who are loving unconditionally need, themselves, to feel well-loved.

Failure of parental love can therefore come from the parents' lack of inner capacity because of their own early experiences, or may be a combination of those and a lack of love and/or protection in the immediate environment. Poverty, bad housing, debts, little support from family and friends, or lack of love from a partner, all make it harder for parents to love in an open unconditional way.

~

Simone had always believed that she would be a 'natural' mother, having had experience of looking after children as a nanny and being a warm and receptive person. Two months before she gave birth to Jason she left work feeling on top of the world. Nigel, her partner, was in a good job, and both agreed that her place should be at home for the early months of the baby's life. Nigel was made redundant just ten days before Jason's birth. Initially they maintained high spirits. Jason was a lovely and easy baby and Nigel was confident that he would soon find work. However, during the next six months this confidence disappeared, along with their savings, and they faced the prospect of their home being repossessed. Nigel became depressed and cut off from both Simone and Jason.

In response to the external trauma around her, Simone also felt depressed, and although she continued to function in a practically nurturing way towards Jason, she ceased to talk to him or enjoy his presence. Jason's verbal skills were still below average two years later. When they were tested, Simone felt a terrible wave of guilt. Things were now looking better for herself and Nigel financially, although their anxieties about security were still high. She had hoped to provide such good and stable mothering for Jason and felt that both he and she had been cheated of this by external circumstances which drained her capacity to love in the short term.

The parents who are struggling in their present lives may find that they actually envy their baby's dependency. Envy is a destructive emotion, which attacks the capacity for expressing love. Sometimes both parents envy the baby, at others one parent envies the relationship between the baby and their partner. Most commonly, the man experiences envy of the close union of mother and baby. Part of the evolving responsibilities of paternal love is to encourage gradual separation of mother and baby. To be healthy this needs to be achieved by the father taking an increasing role in the infant's life, thereby releasing the mother to regain her own emotional boundaries and spend some time free from the demands of the child. When the man envies the closeness of mother and baby, he is liable to force separation too early, responding to his inner needs rather than those of baby and mother. He may also attempt to achieve separation by making increasing demands on the mother to care for him, rather than releasing her from the baby's demands. Such an approach, based in the distortion of his love for her by the envy he is experiencing, is liable to push her into depression, making her less able to meet anyone's needs.

~

Mark found that he could not bear to watch Ginny breastfeeding their baby. It filled him with rage and an overwhelming sense of emptiness and help- lessness. She seemed to give everything to the baby while he felt that he was getting nothing. Lacking the maturity to talk or think about this situation, he simply responded to these inner feelings. He became violent towards Ginny, particularly over mealtimes. His food was never on time, never properly cooked, never arranged in the right way on the plate. Each of these sins became excuses to hit Ginny. Far from encouraging Ginny to love him more, he effectively extinguished the love she had once felt for him. It was only after she had left him that he began to understand just how much envy had destroyed.

~

While maternal love is symbolically enveloping and aimed towards care, nurture and security, much paternal love may be expressed more boisterously. Fathers, like Bobbie in an earlier example, are more liable to throw their children around in play even when quite young. Babies often enjoy this form of excitement without, of course, any thought to possible dangers. Meanwhile mothers have to stand back and watch the baby being tossed around. Knowing when to intervene with a partner's expression of love is a difficult judgement to make. Mothers can be too cloying in their love and fathers too active. In order to develop, the baby needs the experience of security and excitement, of reassurance and challenge, from whichever parent is able to offer these different varieties of love. It is in this early experience of the balance between security and excitement in the love we are offered that we learn a basis which will guide our choice in love partners in the future. Even amongst brothers and sisters, parents may offer a very different balance depending on the sex of the child or their own maturity when that child is born. The quality of the parental relationship may also be reflected in this balance.

Because many children are now born into or raised in one parent families, it is not unusual for one adult to be trying to be many different things to a child. The parent may find that they have to develop aspects of themselves to express love in new ways not previously familiar to them. This usually means fathers learning to be more carefully nurturing and sensitive, and mothers learning to apply firm boundaries and stick to them in the face of infant pressure. While it is exhausting and psychologically stretching to attempt to act as the source of both forms of parental love at the same time, it can also be a time of personal growth for that parent, helping them understand new aspects of relationships generally.

~

Joseph had always considered himself a man's man, but when his wife, Naomi, died giving birth to their second child he was left with little choice but to change. At first his motivation to change was his indebtness to Naomi. With the help of close relatives he learnt to care for his children in a very different way to the earlier care. He expressed this difference as that between his previous responsibility of looking after the family as a group and his new responsibility to care for the needs of each individual child.

This shift of view meant that he was more nurturing and more available to the children than he had been in the previous family structure, while accepting that their external material well-being would suffer somewhat from his change of focus. He had to cope with feeling deskilled, and suffered from a feeling of lack of status as houseperson. However he realized that his gains were in the area of interpersonal relationships. He felt more comfortable with intimacy, and realized that he had developed a more honed intuition about the feelings of others. Later he described his love as having 'softened' and become more embracing, where as previously he would have described it as 'crystal clear and a decisive force in the family'.

~

Joseph's experience demonstrates how much each of us may be pigeonholed in our expression of love because of sexual stereotyping. Learning new ways of expressing love to our children can be a potent source of shifting the boundaries of stereotypes in an emotional rather than intellectual way.

Maturing parental love

The parents' capacity to love has to mature as the baby grows and his or her needs change. As the baby struggles towards independence, firstly of movement, then of bowel and bladder control, then of self-expression through language and play, so the parents' love of that child is faced with new challenges. Most small animals, including babies, have the capacity to make many adults feel the 'aahh, they are lovely' feeling which gets them love and attention. Toddlers and infants, in their struggle for autonomy, often seem quite deliberately less lovable. As it was once expressed to me: 'You yearn for them to walk and they walk straight into trouble; you yearn for them to talk and the first word they really enjoy is "no".'

If the family structure remains intact, this maturing love is in a triangular relationship, within the context of the parents' love for each other. As the baby grows and begins to see that the parents are separate people with a relationship of their own, he or she may come to resent and envy their more adult closeness and begin to fantasize about separating them. Then the love relationships within the triangle become subject to competition, which may strengthen or strain the bonds. Either one or both parents may find themselves loving the child more than each other. This intense love may be expressed in many ways, including a sense of sexual attraction between child and parent. For the child this attraction is a fantasy game they are playing to see how powerful and important they are. They have a need to know that they are acceptably attractive and exciting to one or both parents. Parents who have never suffered abuse them-selves and have a mature understanding of their own boundaries and relationships have little difficulty recognizing the child's fantasy needs in the love relationship. For parents whose own experience at this stage was real sexual activity with their own parents, such boundaries are difficult to achieve. Many abusive parents are too immature emotionally to understand that there should be psychological boundaries in any love relationship.

The sense of appropriate sexuaity is an important parameter in any love attachment. Never is it more crucial than in these moments of sexual love between parent and child. Parents who fear this sexuality and therefore emotionally freeze the child out at this stage can also do damage, and it is something of a narrow line which parents have to tread. Increasingly, parents know this and worry about it, wanting to express love tenderly and physically to their growing children and yet fearing that they might overstep these invisible boundaries. Children, as they explore their own increasing sense of sexuality, can be provocative and can certainly say or do things which would make their parents blanch. It is a time for the parental love to become less 'gut' and instinct and to become more consciously thought about. A child's sexuality should be a sign for the loving parent to accept decreasing physical involvement. This is the moment to learn about letting go, even when it is painful to do so, when you love another.

Parents may seek therapeutic help when they fear that their physical attraction to one or more of their children might be misinterpreted or spill over into demonstrations of affection that feel close to abuse.

~

Jean sought help when her six year old son Graham still wanted to share her bed each night, a habit they had started when he was three and his father had left them. Jean felt increasingly uncomfortable with this, partly because she sensed her own needs for more space and freedom in their relationship, but also because she had felt tempted to reach out and cuddle him for her own satisfaction and re-assurance on several occasions. She felt guilty about this, and repeatedly stated that she would never use him for her own needs in this way. It seemed, to the therapist, that Graham was blocking any hope of his mother making a new sexual relationship by asserting a right to her bed and that although he might not be consciously aware of it, he saw himself as the man of the family who had van-quished the father.

In order for Jean to regain her position as the adult decision-maker in the family, she needed support to make rules and stick to them. For two weeks Graham tried each night, by a variety of ploys, to be allowed access to the bed, but finally gave up. Initially he seemed rather sad and distant to Jean, who felt anxious about whether she had harmed him either by allowing him to stay for so long or by making him go. However, after a short space of time a dramatic change took place, and Graham suddenly started to relate to his peers at school better, get on with work and seemed less anxious and responsible around the house. By re-establishing adult authority firmly, while still clearly loving and caring for Graham, Jean had set him free to be a child rather than the pseudo-man replacement for his father.

~

Increasingly we are being made aware of the range and

extent of sexual abuse within families. While the majority of these cases involve fathers or stepfathers with daughters, mothers also abuse children sexually and fathers sometimes abuse their sons. Grandparents, particularly grandfathers, uncles and family 'friends', may all have access to the child alone which allows them to act on their feelings. While the child may fantasize about sexuality with adults, the reality almost always scares them. The parents manage to convince themselves that they are doing something which the child enjoys as much as they do. They can maintain this belief even in the face of mute horror and physical damage to the child. Such parents are treating the child as if it is a psychological and physical extension of themselves, rather than a separate person with his or her own rights. This form of parental behaviour causes damage to the developing child whose experience of love is being contaminated by betrayal, pain and a simultaneous sense of being unseen while horrifyingly special in relationship to the abusing parent. The parent's capacity for loving another is severely limited, their own needs and desires winning over any other consideration.

Because parental love has to change dramatically over the years in the way it is expressed, there is always the danger that it becomes a role, a duty, responsibility or a job, rather than a feeling. Because the children we have represent a genetic lottery of all our relatives, some parents find themselves in the uncomfortable position of not liking their children, not just on 'off-days' but for prolonged periods of time, maybe for ever. It requires some form of inner assumption on the parent's behalf to continue to love them during these times. For some parents this proves impossible. The demands of parental practicalities sometimes swamp any capacity to continue to love. These parents tend to receive social blame, not just for their neglect but also for the outcome, in terms of the child's behaviour. Most commonly parents are blamed for not nurturing enough in the child's early years or not controlling enough in their growing years. Often parents who fail in one area, fail in the other too, having no model of how to express love creatively to their children from their own parents.

Parents often find that loving their adolescent children is the hardest task of all. By nature adolescence is a time of rejecting parental authority and opinion in favour of that of peers. Parents feel easily hurt and angered by this. Meanwhile they may also find that adolescent desires of their own are stirred up by their children's behaviour. At each stage of the child's development, parents are offered a psychological challenge to re-experience that stage in their own development, but with a more adult mind and a wider range of outcomes. Learning to tolerate the attacks of the offspring in good grace is one of the less rewarding aspects of parental love, but it constitutes a very necessary finishing phase between the love of a dependent child and a new love of a separate and independent adult. Parental love is often most tested by the magnitude of this change.

~

Molly noticed that her parents found it much easier to be loving and supportive of her when she had problems. When her life ran smoothly they had little contact with her. In retrospect she recognized that she had contrived some of her troubles so as to be able to reactivate their caring behaviour. No matter how much she challenged them about this they seemed unable to love her as an independent person, always wishing her back to a younger more dependent state so that they could love her in a way that was unchanged from her childhood.

~

Society too has to look at its role in making parental love easier or harder to express in all of its forms. There is a neverending flow of advice to parents on what constitutes good parenting, but those who volunteer the advice are not around fifteen years later to take the blame for the outcome, whereas the parents are. We do have social blinkers about how mothers and fathers should behave that represent the dominant elements of society's views rather than a healthy overview of many different opinions. For parents, simply to love their children in the context of a social perspective on responsible parenting is hard for many whose intuition may make them wish to express themselves differently. There is a conflict for many parents in bringing children up to 'fit' into society on the one hand or openly express themselves on the other. It is hard to wish to constrict those we love, and yet control is a very important aspect of parental love. As adults we know that those who can never fit in because they lack control will probably live lonely, unsuccessful and unhappy lives.

Mike was an only child who had occupied a central position in his family, both parents focusing all their love on him throughout childhood. When his behaviour caused concern at school his parents would think it was the school's fault. When Mike failed to make friends they felt this was because he was so much brighter than his peers. In early adolescence Mike started to treat his parents with open contempt. At first confused and then deeply hurt by this, both parents felt incapable of making any attempts to stop the behaviour. Regularly in trouble with the police for an escalating series of crimes, Mike was unable to take any responsibility, believing that whatever went wrong was someone else's fault. Although his parents had undoubtably loved him as a child, neither could cope with or understand him as an adolescent. Both felt secretly that they had bred a monster but could not understand why such a loved child had turned out to be so difficult. When a family therapist suggested that Mike needed a firm controlling parental presence in his life, both parents felt that this was the role of the other: neither could imagine risking their perceived perfect love by discipline. Eventually Mike was taken into care because he was felt to be out of control. A firm and rather charismatic house leader gave Mike his first experience of being contained and controlled, and his behaviour improved and his school work, for years neglected, suddenly became important to him.

The conflicts between being the loving parent and the controlling parent come to the fore in loving adolescent children. At this age the child believes him or herself to be more adult than parents usually experience them. Quite often children repeat aspects of their parents' lives which the parents have come, over the years, to regard as mistakes. Dropping out of education can seem like a wonderful freedom to a sixteen-year-old, but how does a loving parent, who did the same thing years earlier and then had a hard struggle later in life, behave or advise? Parents know that the world has as many knocks as adventures and, out of love, we wish to secure the children from those knocks. The teenager can all too easily experience that as rigidity, boredom, lack of understanding and have little or no concept of the fear parents experience for them.

Love at this stage seems to need to be elastic. Having put their children's welfare first for many years, their love may be exhausted and unready for these final hurdles. How to find the balance between holding and letting go is a daily exercise in loving a teenager. When to open your mouth and when to hold your tongue comes to feel like an impossible guessing game. Love can seem like a painful ache, an echo of previous feelings. You want them to go away and yet grieve as they go. The love is being painfully stretched so as to be ready for the new adult-to-adult relationship.

~

Maxine argued with her mother, Marjorie, almost every day for the years between being twelve and fifteen. Marjorie often felt exhausted by this and also increasingly angry and resentful. The men in the family tended to keep out of the way of the women arguing, which made Marjorie feel she was trapped alone with Maxine. Meanwhile Maxine felt confused, anxious about life, worried that she would not cope with exams and finding a boyfriend. She could not share these worries with her mother because she felt, subconsciously, highly competitive with her. She envied her mother's apparent ability to cope satisfactorily with life, and secretly doubted whether she could ever do the same. At fifteen, after a brief relationship with a boyfriend whom her parents had disliked, she discovered that she was pregnant. Although her doctor advised her to discuss this with her parents, Maxine could not bring herself to do this, imagining that they would throw her out, or at least humiliate her in some way. Instead her behaviour deteriorated until she was screaming at her mother for hours on end about perceived slights and old hurts.

Marjorie suddenly found herself reliving arguments she had had with her own mother. She remembered how cut off from the adults she had felt and how much her angry shouting had been an attempt to communicate across the perceived gulf. She stopped shouting back and tried to listen to what Maxine was saying, even though this was painful for her. Meanwhile Maxine felt the difference in her mother's reaction and started to cry rather than shout. Throughout the coming weeks,

Maxine's abortion and the subsequent ups and downs, Marjorie felt set free from their previous relationship and able to care for her daughter as an adult. Many years later, Maxine told her mother how grateful she had been that there had never been any reproach or blame from her mother. It was surprisingly easy for Marjorie to say that Maxine had, in her eyes, become a woman and at that moment of change in her perception of her daughter a new relationship had started.

~

Adult children

Perhaps the best test of parental love is in the relationship child and parent make, adult to adult. Can they find a form of equality in respect, care, concern, enjoyment of each other, or does the necessary inequality of these feelings from earlier years pervade the grown-up relationship? Once the child becomes an adult there can be a delightful shedding of the sense of responsibility for his or her well-being. Support can be offered from one adult to another, and not from one who is independent to one still perceived as dependent. The child may change away from home and develop aspects of themselves concealed at home. And the child will experience the knocks of life, make the mistakes and experience some sadness, not least in their own relationships with their own children. Parental love often needs to have acquired wisdom and a sense of peace with itself by this stage to be non-intrusively present. The child may not allow a parental presence and cause much anguish to the loving parent. A happy ending to the process of parenting is a momentary experience, and a few minutes later the relationship asks for us to meet a new challenge, the love never ceasing to change from beginning to end.

One of the most important aspects of loving is a capacity to allow the loved one to love you and care for you too. Children need space to express this throughout childhood, by gifts, expressions and practical caring. Their parents' reactions to this love returned is an important part of the feedback loop between parent and child. This loop becomes more sophisticated in adult to adult relating, when the grown-up child may have a greater ability to care for the parent than the parent retains to care for them. This swapping of the balance of dependency can be a difficult negotiation, or it can grow to help support an ageing parent, who now loves their child with respect born out of very different needs to those in the earlier days of their relationship.

~

Although Sid had dreaded old age and dependency on his son, he was surprised to find that he was grateful to move in with their family. Two years as a widower had left him lonely, bored, and not looking after himself well. Now he felt a new motivation, surrounded by their love and enthusiasm. He realized that although he was increasingly dependent on his son and daughter-in-law, he still had a family role to play. At the pensioners club he would boast about his son's success, feeling well justified in his pride and knowing that the love he had felt for the small baby he had held forty years earlier had come full circle round to him feeling held by his son.

~

For the child, parental love can be like good compost in which to grow. For the parent, the experience of that love, in all its forms, may make an important contribution to their own pathway towards greater emotional maturity.

4

Love Between Brothers and Sisters

Sibling love/sibling rivalry

Parents are often encouraged to prepare first or subsequent children for the arrival of a new baby brother or sister. We understand that not all feelings between siblings are loving and accepting. Nevertheless, the bond between brothers and sisters can be remarkably strong, given that these are bonds based in genetic resemblance and a sharing of that most crucially defining part of our lives, our childhood.

Siblings share parents. In this they share an experience which, although never identical, since parents always treat children slightly differently, is similar. They are also witness to the childhood of each other. This sharing can bond them to each other with an understanding that connects them whatever their future relationships are.

Although close as children, Simon and Jackie saw little of each other in early adult life as both married and raised young children. Living at opposite ends of the country meant that they had little time to exchange news, and one family Christmas when they did have time together both were surprised and distressed to discover how little they seemed to have in common. However, five years later, as both were surviving traumatic divorces, they came together again and rediscovered all their previous closeness. They were able from this trusted position to help each other understand much more about the failed marriages than other adults they confided in seemed able to do.

~

The common experience of sharing parents is never an entirely easy process. Envy of the love that is demonstrated for a sibling can devastate family life.

~

Clementine was five when her brother, Louis, was born. Although her parents tried to prepare her for his arrival, she remained uninterested, fully occupied by starting school and making new friends. However, as soon as Louis came home with mother from the hospital, Clementine became demanding and unhappy. Both parents were surprised by this, and rather than understanding her difficulties in accepting a new 'rival' for their affections, became critical of and hostile to her behaviour. She was given the message that she was only acceptable to them as their 'lovely little girl' if she loved her brother. In order to conform she became 'loving' and would cuddle him and push his pram around the garden. Both parents congratulated themselves on having resolved the problem rapidly, without realizing that they had only changed Clementine's external behaviour. Inside she still seethed with rage and harboured murderous fantasies about Louis.

Repression of her feelings had the added problem of her now feeling guilty and shameful about herself and her feelings. Over the years, Clementine watched for signs of favouritism so as to justify her inner feelings. Any child watching especially for such signs will always find many examples in family life, but in this family Louis probably was given certain advantages simply because he was a boy. Thus her catalogue of grievances grew and her envy and hatred of her brother grew too.

~

Such toxic situations often fester in families for many years, occasionally breaking out in fights or accusations, but otherwise 'underground' until the children reach adolescence or adulthood. Clearly they are much more likely to occur in families where one child does occupy a favoured position over the other. However, even in families that struggle hard to maintain equality in their treatment of the children, one child may still come to feel especially disadvantaged compared to the others.

Envy is profoundly destructive. When we feel envy we wish to destroy rather than possess. Thus if we envy a sibling our prime goal is to eliminate him or her, either through murderous fantasies or by discrediting them to parents. Because destruction is the prime goal, the love of the parent, however warmly given, does not take away the hateful sensations towards the brother or sister.

Envy is also an emotion connected to an early part of infant development. When, as infants, we envied our mother's capacity to feed and nurture us, we harboured similarly destructive fantasies about her, which may get transferred onto a newly-arrived sibling. It may feel safer to envy the new baby rather than the mother. However, in developmental terms we grow to a position when we begin to worry about having possibly damaged mother with our fantasies, feeling a sense of responsibility and guilt for what we imagined and a desire to make it better, to make reparation. This is an important step in developing a sense of responsibility for our behaviour within all future relationships. If we transfer our envy from mother to sibling before we have worked through to a place where we wish to make amends then, developmentally, we may become stuck.

~

This proved to be the case for Clementine, who remained envious of her brother throughout childhood and spent much of her adult life trying to beat Louis at various activities rather than do the things which would have fulfilled herself. Strangely, despite her attacks and competitive stance, Louis loved Clementine and thought her brave and rebellious, in ways that he had never dared to be. It took this sister and brother fifty years to find time to sit down and listen to each other's experience and perception of life: time they found in the two weeks it took them to sort out their parents' affairs after their death, together, in an accident.

~

Sibling jealousy

Brothers and sisters can also feel jealousy rather than love. Most often a brother feels jealousy of a sister's loved position in father's eyes while a sister feels similarly about a brother's position in his mother's affections. These feelings arise from a later stage of development than the envious ones and are concerned with sexual attraction between two people of which a third can feel excluded and therefore jealous.

As the prime goal of jealousy is to possess the loved one or capture the love and attention of the one we wish to love us, it produces different forms of behaviour, in which we compete for what we want without primarily thinking that we need to destroy our competitors. Thus brothers and sisters often compete for parental attention when younger, and external success when older. Within normal parameters in the context of an otherwise loving and secure family this is often channelled into games and activities in which competition can flourish safely and be a source of entertainment and fun. In less secure families, such competition can become too serious, too intense a source of pleasure for the winner and despair for the loser. This is sometimes the case in families where the parents are still driven by sibling competition which they have transferred into their marriage, thereby modelling ongoing competition rather than cooperation to the children.

Adult siblings

From these examples it becomes obvious that, because sibling love has to flourish when both parties are still in the early days of their own development, it is a love which can be deeply rooted or deeply troubled. For many brothers and sisters it is a complex mixture of the two, a loving relationship in which they feel enmeshed but uncertain. The pattern of relating established in childhood will probably remain into adulthood: thus the bossy elder child may retain a sense of having the right to interfere in 'baby' brother or sister's life. The youngest may feel that they will always be looked after. The eldest may carry a weight of responsibility.

The position in which we are born, first, second, middle or third child, often also allocates us a role in family life. Thus a first child often has to carry many more parental expectations than subsequent children. In many ways first children get parents who are new and untrained and who 'practise' parenting on them before being rather more relaxed and sophisticated in their parenting skills with the next baby. A middle child may have to fight to have a role, the old notion of an heir and a spare leaving the 'spare' one with a vacuum of expectation. The last child in a family may be allowed to develop independent skills later than previous children, as if the whole family wants to maintain them in baby mode for as long as possible. These roles often present problems in the relationships between brothers and sisters because they are allocated to each of us based on external parameters rather than being rooted in our natural skills and enthusiasms.

~

Robert, as first-born son, was expected to do well at school and go to university. He struggled through secondary education, often feeling unhappy and out of his depth, but his parents refused to believe that he was not capable if he just 'tried harder'. Meanwhile, his younger sister, Melanie, whose education received little attention from her parents, sailed through in top streams for all subjects, apparently effortlessly. Melanie was a great supporter of Robert, who she had idealized since she was an infant and it troubled her to see him failing at things she considered easy. She was also uncomfortable with her successes even though little praise came her way. She was aware that 'for the family' it was only Robert's achievements that counted. This situation, ignoring these children's different abilities, left both uneasy and confused. They often confided in each other, and found their major support in their sibling relationship which increasingly 'cut out' parental messages. It is not surprising that the parents found the behaviour of both of their children disappointing, indeed they had in effect 'set them up' to be a disappointment. This had been both parents' experience of their own childhood too, and so their experience as parents had a *déjà vu* quality to it.

Robert and Melanie continued to love and support each other throughout adult life, both much more in tune with the other's innate qualities. As brother and sister they shared the most unconditional love either ever received. Although this had been important in helping them survive during childhood, it became an obstacle to their future relationships.

~

Siblings and gender

One of the biggest stumbling blocks for brother and sister love is the experience, still surprisingly common, that boys are valued more, or at least differently, to girls. This experience seems to start from the moment the midwife declares 'it's a girl' or 'it's a boy'. The parents' previous assumptions about the baby become instantly gender-fixed and, for many parents, a girl brings disappointment. In some parts of the world, particularly if parents are only allowed one child, a girl baby will be abandoned or killed. Cultures in which a girl child spells dire financial consequences also kill their female infants. Although these murders are the response to cultural pressures, it is important to remember that the adults concerned are those responsible for defining and continuing that culture. Therefore they are not, as they experience themselves to be, powerless in these lethal choices. If it can be acted out in any culture then some semblance of the fantasy must be present in all of our inner worlds.

We can, at least, comfort ourselves that we do not kill baby girls in the western world. However all research suggests that parents often do experience the birth of a daughter, particularly as a first child, as a disappointment and that girl infants are held less, breast-fed for shorter times, stimulated less and perceived as less 'needy' than their brothers. Even parents who have struggled to give their offspring equality find it hard to fight against both external and internal messages and assumptions that are laid down in the annals of the history of inequality.

Freud talked of penis envy as if little girls would be phallocentric in their orientation. However, by the time a girl becomes sexually aware of the bodily differences in her brother she will have already had several years experience of inequality, both in her own experience and her vision of her mother's. That being the case, she has a great deal more than just his penis to envy in her brother. Such envy is not of the same sort as envy of an internal characteristic or capability of another. But rather a sociocultural rage at unfairness and injustice which is second nature, although often deeply repressed, in sisters for their brothers. In the 1990s we like to think that the toxin of inequality has been neutralized and everything will be much easier for sisters in relationship to their brothers in future generations. And yet in almost every home, whether or not mother earns a living or indeed is the major bread-winner for the family, she will still be seen to be also the major 'servicer' of the needs of others, both practical and emotional. In such a climate, the little girl still has a frightening vision of femaleness with which to identify. The sister may make less fuss when pressed to do domestic tasks than her brother, and the mother, who has already given up hope of sharing equal domestic responsibility with a male in her own life, may be easily tempted to press the daughter to do more while her brother does less.

While there may be an argument for little girls being, mostly, genuinely quieter and less disruptive, liking dolls, cooperative play and nurturing as the early signs of them acquiring maternal skills, there can be no biological argument for them doing more housework than their brothers. Nature does not provide little girls with special dishwasher-stacking or ironing hands. However, it does make girls naturally competitive with their mothers, and if mothers are still unpaid domestic servants then the girl will compete in that arena without any idea of how entrapping such behaviour is.

If a girl is more of a house-servant than her brother she may feel resentment, she may also feel rather superior, as if she is more grown-up and responsible than him. This pattern of feelings, resentment and defensive superiority, is then likely to be mirrored in all her future relationships with men who are her peers. Many women maintain this dual position in which they defend against their underlying fury about inequality by believing themselves to be more superior and grown-up than men. I have never seen a man fight against this. It suits them fine to have all domestic tasks cared for while they rest and play. And how does the sister, the wife, even the female flatmate cope with her anger, rage and sadness if she dares to see that she is simply an unpaid servant. Being a servant cannot be superior and being unpaid is certainly not very grown-up!

Inequality will, for as long as it exists in any form, make the love between brothers and sisters difficult. Therefore in adult love we are more likely to talk of brother-love or sister-love for those within the same-sex group, because this has less hidden assumptions. If we say 'he loves her like a brother' or 'she loves him like a sister' we are usually defining an asexual adult relationship which has hidden assumptions of duty and responsibilities.

In many cultures in which the extended family is still a major social building block, the relationship between brother and sister is more crucial to social stability than that between husband and wife. Primary loyalties run deeply in such relationships, expressed in both emotional and material ways. Thus a woman's strength and importance, initially defined by her father's position and role, will come in adult life to depend on the number and position of her brothers. Their deaths will have a social as well as personal significance for her. Such relationships of honour, duty and obligation, although usually expressed as love, must also have an undercurrent stemming from basic inequalities which erodes the potential love.

Sibling abuse

Love between brothers and sisters can become physical. Children who live closely together and who play together will, of course, be in physical proximity with each other for years on end. In children's games the observation and examination of each others' bodies plays a part, and brothers and sisters indulge in such games even more commonly than friends do. At what point does the innocence of children's fantasy and play slip into sibling abuse? Generally speaking the larger the age gap and the greater the degree of coercion or force the more abusive the experience is. Abuse happens brother to sister, brother to brother and sister to brother, although the latter is probably more rare.

~

Suzy used to lock herself in the toilet when her parents went out so that her brother, Tom, could not attack her. From the age of seven she feared going to sleep in case she woke to find him in her bed. He claimed to be teaching and helping her but threatened that the parents would side with him if she told anyone. By the age of eleven he was regularly forcing her to have intercourse and this continued until she became pregnant at fourteen. Tom was nineteen at the time and denied all Suzy's accusations. He blamed her for trying to break up the family, and as he had always predicted, the family sided with him. In later teenage Suzy took several overdoses and cut her wrists in what she described as attempts to exorcize Tom from her body. Tom used these occasions to impress on his parents just how mad Suzy was.

~

Parents are often ignorant about the nature of the rela-

tionships between their children, especially during adolescence when much is hidden from them. They may
have started out with high hopes that their children
would all be loving and supportive to each other and
therefore turn a blind eye to the reality of the situation.
Parents who have been only-children themselves tend to
be particularly over-hopeful about the nature of sibling
relationships, and the ferocity of their own children's
battles may take them by surprise. Parents with children
who are handicapped in some way often overestimate the
degree to which the siblings have adapted to this situation. For many children, the experience of having a sick
or restricted brother or sister leaves them with all the
normal turbulent emotions of sibling love but without
any permission or possibility of expressing such feelings,
even feeling guilty about having them. This may be the
template for a pattern of relating to 'sick' friends in
adult life.

~

Everyone thought that Marianne was the ideal
person to become a nurse, as she had had so much
experience of helping her mother look after her
brother, who had suffered serious brain damage at
birth. Marianne was amazed and distressed to discover that far from liking her patients she rapidly
came to resent them and even envy their 'sick'
position in which they seemed to get care and
attention. All the feelings for her brother, deeply
repressed during childhood, surfaced in her relationship with patients. With support Marianne was

able to see that there was no disgrace in giving up on nursing as a career. Her feelings were a natural and human, rather than evil, response to her childhood experiences, where she had certainly received less than her fair share of adult love and attention.

~

Clearly, then, brother and sister love can be as complex as any other form of love, intensified by it being a peer relationship conducted as both or all parties are still going through early developmental stages. Such love is conceived in the context of family and social constraints, duties and obligations which both bolster and erode its true potential. Often we say of friends 'I love you like a sister or brother' and this is meant to be a compliment. However, we do not, cannot, chose our siblings, or even how many of them there are, and even if we disown them and they are far away they will also still reside inside of us as developmental mementoes of earlier days.

5

Love and Sexuality

The relationship between love and sexuality is one which has been much argued. During the process of development, physical, emotional and spiritual, we all interweave aspects of love and our sexuality differently. This leads to confusion between lovers and sometimes great conflict within a person. Society and religion have attempted to lay down rules, which are meant to minimize such conflict and confusion, but have been notoriously unsuccessful at helping individuals understand their own or their partners' needs and desires, behaviour and emotions.

Sexuality and the breast

Libido is a Latin word meaning 'need' or 'desire'. It was first used by Freud to describe sexual energy. He saw that such an energy was intrinsic to us all from early childhood. As his theories advanced, he connected this energy with the life instinct which pushes each of us towards survival: an instinct which is always at odds with its opposite, the death instinct. Also connected to the life instinct and libido is the need for pleasure.

Marie, born and raised in Caen, France, met Christopher while studying languages at Exeter University. They fell passionately in love within hours of first meeting. This intensely physical relationship made both feel more alive than they had ever felt before. Both seemed to glow with an inner light which further fed for each of them their attraction to the other. Such intense 'living' is often the experience of those who are in the first flush of passion and love. After a particularly orgasmic evening, Marie used a French phrase of having experienced 'a little death' to describe the peak of their passion. Christopher felt a tremor of excitement to realize that they were riding on some edge along which the experience of both life and death were merged.

~

During early childhood, the prime motive of the baby sucking at the breast is for food, nutrition – survival. However, the baby has a range of emotional and physical experiences during that sucking, some of which are helping the infant develop an understanding of the emotion of love and some of which are arousing and pleasurable, the beginnings of oral sexuality. The sensations the baby experiences around the lips and tongue are his or her first experiences of focusing the sexual libidinal energy onto an organ. Infants will often continue to suck after the bottle is empty or the need for milk from the breast is long satisfied, simply because it is pleasurable and reassuring. This form of behaviour holds the key to many of the emotional arenas which cause such conflict in adult sexuality, as well as providing the template for what is usually the first, and questionably the most intimate sexual activity – kissing.

By using the breast for pleasure and reassurance the infant is also demonstrating some form of control and power over an organ which in fact has the power of life and death over him or her. For the early months, the breast, or its substitute the bottle, is the part of the mother (or mother-substitute) upon which the baby's energies are concentrated. The breast can satisfy or frustrate, and thus the baby can love and idealize it or hate and denigrate it. The preoccupation with breasts as sexual objects in the western world stems back to such early developmental experiences. As adults, men use power (often symbolized by money) to make sure that there is a ready availability of breasts, so that they never need to feel the helplessness, powerlessness and threat that a withholding breast arouses in the infant.

Such pornography may reassure and even satisfy, much as the first breast experienced had the power to do. Much of this form of pornography exaggerates the importance of big breasts as symbols of the possibility of overwhelming satisfaction. The men who enjoy such pictures always say that it only constitutes harmless fun. However, it is undoubtedly infantile pleasure that they are seeking at a primate level, and dangers of such pornography occur when, far from reassuring and satisfying, the image of the breast stirs up distant memories of hate, rage and denigration. Within these emotions often lie the fantasies of attack of the envied breast, including its destruction. Then, far from being harmless fun such pictures provoke powerfully hostile feelings towards breasts, and by generalization, towards women.

Men can never own the powerful feeding breast as part of their own body, and as such it may be a potent external symbol of the stunning creative powers of a woman's body which they envy and wish to attack and destroy, or own and dominate. Most women understand this danger, either consciously or unconsciously. Some use it to provoke within safe limits, others make money by pushing those limits to dangerous places, while the majority worry about their breasts, the size, the shape and whether to cover or uncover, restrict or flaunt them. In many ways the anxieties of women about their breasts often mirror their greater, more existential, anxieties about whether they should own, use and flaunt any powerful aspect of themselves. Fear of men's envy is often a forceful consideration in the dilemma.

For women, who also experience, as infants, the whole range of mixed emotions of oral arousal at the breast and a love/hate relationship with it, there is the added complication of growing into a woman who herself has breasts. The powerful organ, once fantasized as being part of her and then during development recognized as part of mother, during adolescence once again becomes part of herself. Adolescent girls often demonstrate a preoccupation with the rate of development of their breasts, as if it is their only advantageous feature. But they are surrounded by a culture both fascinated and threatened by the power of the breast, a power which seems to have been curiously enhanced rather than diminished by the high rate of bottle-feeding in the last to or three generations.

Many a story tells us that if a girl withholds genital sex then she may intensify her male's desires to such a point that he will give her anything she wants; usually, in romantic fiction, marriage. Perhaps the generations of mothers who have for many reasons withheld their breasts from their infants have also raised the level of frustration/desire associated with them. In reality many women do not breastfeed their infants because of the confusions in society about the purpose and function of their breasts. In the western world, we do not encourage breastfeeding in public, as if it were a socially dangerous activity rather than a nurturing necessity. Women often puzzle over who owns their breasts and whether they are primarily nurturing or sexual organs. The opinions of their male partners often dominate such reflections, at the cost of the needs of their offspring. Because of this, many a mother then also has to cope with a sense of guilt for not having breastfed.

~

Kristina went to her doctor with post-natal depression when her son, Harry, was ten weeks old. She told the doctor that she had 'failed' Harry by deciding to stop breastfeeding, despite all the advice and encouragement she had received to carry on. Having read leaflets and babycare books, she knew that she had 'ruined' Harry's life already and that he would have emotional problems, less resistance to infection and a higher risk of cot death. In view of all this, the doctor queried why she had decided to stop. She explained that her boyfriend could not bear to be in the same room as herself and Harry when she was feeding him and became angry, even explosive, if she tried to raise the problem. Since starting Harry on bottles she described the tension in their home as considerably reduced, although the father's envy of Harry was still evident.

The GP reminded her of how, in previous generations, baby books would always include a section on 'reassuring Dad', who may 'feel left out'.

~

We expect fathers to be more grown-up and involved as adults in the process of childrearing these days, but for many men this appears to be demanding too much for their emotional limits. Breastfeeding is often the first arena in which the father demonstrates his limits of tolerance and the extent of his envy. The man who expects to be able to buy his breasts for the cost of a daily newspaper, for instance, may not take kindly to sharing his partner's breasts with a new-born infant. As a society we encourage his view that breasts are his for the buying, rather than support the struggling mother to consider her own needs while she is in conflict between the emotional needs of her baby and her partner. The mother's depression is the price of being the owner of the fought-over breasts.

Whatever the reasons for our western preoccupation with breasts, it affects men and women very differently.

For both men and women the nipples and breast tissues are physiologically erogenous zones, they contain erectile tissue which responds to touch, temperature, even our thoughts and feelings This arousal response is often more intense in women: indeed many a sexually active man, who would consider himself an adventurous lover, feels strangely uncomfortable with arousal based on his nipples. The stimulation of nipples is a complex inter-action of a here-and-now physiological response, com-bined with distant undertones of the memories of early development for both partners. Thus, while being physi-cally exciting for one partner, say the woman, who is both being aroused by physical stimulation and mental association, the male partner may be experiencing the foreplay in a number of ways, enjoyable or anxiety-pro-voking. His fingertips or lips may also be experiencing physical excitation; he may be idealizing the breast, adoring it, enjoying dominating it, intellectually enjoying pleasing his partner; or he may be worried by it, wanting to bite and hurt rather than love and enjoy.

Giving the breast pleasure may be a wonderfully releasing experience for a man who, as a child, felt dominated by the breast. Or he may relive that early infantile experience of pleasure at the breast in his sucking, thereby activating deeply primitive experiences of dependency. However, there is often an element of the sado-masochistic in such foreplay. The relationship with the breast is not straightforward, for any child, male or female. Thus the pleasurable sucking can easily change to nipping and biting, which sadistically is equally satisfying and arousing. The desire to give pleasure may be only a hair's breadth away from an equal desire to cause pain and to dominate or denigrate. Much pathologically sadistic behaviour focuses on hurting, damaging, even destroying the breast.

Women have the same emotional resonances from childhood suckling, but as the breasts are part of them there is a stronger possibility that their arousal will be increased by a masochistic desire to push the barrier between pain and pleasure. In the heights of arousal, particularly if inhibitions are released by alcohol or drugs, for instance, there is always the danger that sado-masochism will go beyond safe limits. Clearly the less dominant or least physically powerful partner is more at risk in this situation.

Pain and pleasure

Men have been said to be the only sex to experience sexual perversions. It has taken the recent work of the analyst Estela Welldon to point out that men act out their perversion against external objects or partners, while women are much more likely to act against themselves. This is because they strongly identify their own body with the body of their mother, with whom the original developmental experience occurred.

Attacks on breasts not only occur in the enactment of sexual fantasy, but are also sometimes enacted within the bounds of accepted social normality. Thus surgeons thought it normal and absolutely right to treat breast cancer by an excision of all the breast and muscular tissue of the chest wall. No matter that women hated this treatment and were often as deeply scarred psychologically as physically by it, it was seen as necessary because it was life-saving. It took much research and many years to demonstrate that simply removing the lump and leaving the remainder of the breast as little scarred as possible was equally life-saving. Surgeons were interestingly resistant to this research and its results.

Historically, women have bound and mutilated their own breasts in a variety of ways, both to be socially acceptable and quite possibly to fulfil sado-masochistic needs of their own. I have often wondered about the explanation of the Amazons cutting off a breast in order to make it easier for them to fire a bow and arrow more accurately. Any woman who has ever tried archery knows that this is, at best, a flimsy excuse for such a radical measure. More likely that the psyche of women as the dominant sex in a culture required some sacrifice of their identification with and their sadism towards their birthmothers, and that a breast was that sacrifice.

Some lesbians have commented that they think heterosexual women project much if not all of their sadism into the men they relate to, while maintaining their masochism. It may be that in cultures where women are still dominated by men they have no choice but to perform such psychological acrobatics. Meanwhile, lesbians acknowledge that sado-masochism exists within their sexuality, sometimes split so that sadism is only expressed by one partner and masochism in the other, sometimes shared between partners, in a way that causes homosexuality for women to be a profoundly different and perhaps more complex psychological experience than heterosexuality.

For heterosexual women, the sexual equivalent of the sucking experience with its infantile sexuality at the breast may be re-experienced by oral sex with their male partners. The penis is then experienced as the nipple as well as their partner's genital organ, and the same mixed desires for pleasuring and paining exists. These powerful and arousing psychological experiences, which enhance the physiological arousal, may stay as a fantasy within the individual, or may be a shared fantasy with the partner, or may be acted out physically across a wide range of both normality and perversion.

There is an interesting degree of overlap of such fantasies between men and women, based in our shared early developmental experiences. One example of such fantasy (I think it was fantasy!) was a story I heard from both a woman campaigner at Greenham Common and from an American soldier at the base. Both claimed that they had been told that this fantasy had actually happened, although there was no real evidence that it had occurred. It involved a soldier who, in order to humiliate a campaigner, had poked his penis through the wire fence with instructions to the campaigner as to what she should do with it. While pretending to fellate the man in line with his suggestions, the campaigner bit it off. Both the man and woman who told me this story, literally from opposite sides of the fence, appeared much aroused by it, with gestures and laughter which suggested an excited horror.

Sex vs love

The degree to which love is the safeguard against the

expression of sado-masochism as a perversion, or a horror, can only be postulated. During early development there is undoutably much potential for a physical war of the sexes, which is transformed by our experiences of love, security and respect into a more hopeful and safe passion. It is the potential for opening up early infantile experiences by our sexuality which make sex an intimate act with a trusted partner. Sex which is just about arousal and excitation may well be more immediately exciting, without the inhibitions and safeguards that love is likely to place on our acting-out of fantasy; it is also inherently more dangerous, psychologically and physically, to both partners.

~

Nicole had had a number of relationships with men who she described as 'using' her. There was a satisfaction in that description. Nicole idealized her own mother who was seen as a remarkably giving woman 'used' by all the family and yet Nicole, while trying to imitate this 'generous-hearted' mother, was also deeply unhappy about the psychological state that each of these relationships left her in. She related stories of how she fed these men, not just with food but with money, time and emotional support. During sex she said that she was most aroused if the men sucked her nipples so hard that it caused her pain and left bruising: it was at that point during intercourse when she felt most powerful and good about herself. Genital intercourse was always a disappointment, it was an act

in which she felt disinterest and she often reverted
to thinking about shopping or the next meal while
her partners penetrated her.

Each of these relationships ran a similar course,
with the men 'sucking her dry' and then leaving,
often with criticisms about Nicole's lack of femininity. Such words hurt Nicole deeply, as she
believed herself to be the epitome of femininity as
observed in her mother. 'But I give them everything,' she said, puzzled as to why they could ever
leave.

~

Nicole is an example of someone who is using aspects of
sexuality as if they were love. She is limited to an oral
understanding and experience of sexuality, without any
real self-esteem or concept of emotional love beyond
simple nurturing of a dependent other (in which she
assumes that they too only have oral needs). Her identification with her mother had made her peculiarly vulnerable to any partner who wanted to abuse her.

~

Barry has also experienced many relationships. He
boasts to his friends about the number of his conquests, while bemoaning to his therapist how
deeply unsatisfied he often feels. During his early
life he was fostered by a number of families, each
of which took good care of him. However, he was
more than two before adoption could be arranged.
His attitude to women had been learnt by this

earlier experience of multiple care, in that he saw them as a collection of organs which met this basic needs without any grasp of the fact that they might be complete people who could satisfy him more emotionally as well as physically. During the early months of his first committed relationship he became depressed as he began to understand what had been missing emotionally in his early care.

～

Barry is an example of someone who has not had early opportunities to begin to experience arousal and satisfaction within the context of a secure and continuing loving relationship. Thus later adult sexuality was also cut-off from any understanding of his emotional needs (or the emotions of others).

Our developing capacity for love grows alongside other psychological development. By the age of two the child learns that he or she can gain pleasure and arousal from other organs. Many children clearly enjoy contact with pleasant feeling materials and their skin, for instance, at an early age. During the second and third years of life, as the child is learning sphincter control, in both urination and defacation, they are also learning that there is a sensual pleasure as well as an excretive one, to be gained from exercising these sphincters. This discovery may be the first time that their focus of sensual attention is in the area of their genitalia, although most analysts believe that children are aware of the sensual potential of genitalia earlier, perhaps even being born with that awareness.

Urinary sphincters and the anus now become the organs of most excitement to the child. Arousal associated with these organs is connected to the emotional struggles for control and autonomy that the child is waging, both with external authority figures and with his or her own body. Issues of power, control and autonomy are important in all loving relationships. It is often arguments in one or more of these areas which lead couples to 'turn off' their potential sexual arousal As Carl G. Jung commented,'Where love rules, there is no will to power: and where power predominates, the love is lacking. the one is the shadow of the other.'

~

Brian and Zaida had been married for five years. Their sexual relationship had been satisfying for them both until an argument about the control of their finances had led Zaida to feel sexually cold and uninterested. 'I'm not punishing him,' she said. 'My body really does seem to have "turned off" because I feel so dominated and out of control of my life.'

~

It is clear that most adults need to feel a degree of true adult control over themselves and their lives in order to be able to 'let go' sexually. Power is accepted as a potent aphrodisiac, but usually seen as attractive in men and somewhat frightening in women. However, women often have to have a sense of their own power before they can realize the full potential of their sexuality. This may explain why women often report feeling more sexy in their thirties and forties, when they are more self-assured, than at a younger age.

Gay men and lesbians

Anal-centred sexuality remains a possibility for both men and women. It can be both physiologically and psychologically arousing. Many societies have sought to outlaw anal intercourse, either heterosexual or homosexual, presumably because the defacation function of the anus inspires fears about contamination and illness. In recent years, the spread of AIDS has underlined these fears; the rectal mucosa is not as strong as vaginal mucosa, and thus is more easily torn and damaged. This leaves the body open to infection.

Fears about male homosexuality, usually felt most strongly by heterosexual men, often focus on the sense of disgust or shame such men attribute to anal intercourse. However, many heterosexual men enjoy anal intercourse with female partners, despite laws against this practice. For many, it represents a cheap form of contraception.

Most recipients of anal sex report some arousal, but not of the degree likely to lead to orgasm without other stimulation, for example of the penis or clitoris. Psychologically there may be excitement in the concept of the forbidden nature of anal intercourse and, rather more pathologically, some recipients feel aroused by a degree of humiliation connected with being dominated and controlled by another.

In the heyday of gay bath-houses in the United States,

most participants described a rapid series of sexual encounters which did not imply any form of relationship with the other, let alone any love. Although experienced as physically highly arousing, even addictive, such experiences did not satisfy other human needs. There were clear sado-masochistic elements in many of the sexual practices, which you might expect to find in this rather disconnected form of sexuality. The majority of male homosexuals would wish to embed their sexuality within a loving relationship as they mature. Society's prohibitions on their activities continue to make it harder for such relationships to be secured and open, either at work or recreation.

Female homosexuality continues to arouse less fear than the male counterpart. Society expects women to love and care for each other, cuddle and support and talk intimately with each other. Thus the further intimacy of sexuality seems to be less surprising in women than in men. Lesbianism seems to promote a rather less aggressively promiscuous sexuality than male homosexuality, although homosexual relationships share problems of lack of stability and security for both men and women, probably because society does nothing to support them.

～

Jenna felt deeply aroused by Sally's presence. She knew that Sally was 'out' as a lesbian but feared exploring her own sexuality as a homosexual. This produced a conflict in her mind, between satisfying her instinctual physical needs and experiencing much-needed love within a relationship, and a fear that she would become unacceptable to her parents and brother, thereby losing the relationships she most depended on for love and support. Eventually the psychological conflict made her physically ill, and she avoided any decision by accepting a job in the United States, thus distancing her from the 'temptation' which Sally's presence offered. Obviously, such a partial solution will only hold the conflict at bay for a while, and cannot protect Jenna from long-term dilemmas about her sexuality.

~

Our fears about homosexuality probably rest in Freud's contention that most of us are fundamentally bisexual. We conform to society's norms for a quite life, but live with the fears, usually unconscious, that a homosexual encounter might be more exciting than we dare experience. Kinsey suggested that a mere 10 per cent at each end of the spectrum are absolutely homosexual or absolutely heterosexual, and that the remainder make choices, both consciously and unconsciously, about the sexuality they prefer. If we believe that the majority have a choice over sexual orientation then this choice is probably informed by our previously acquired sense of gender identity as well as from arousal responses to external stimuli. Certainly children between the age of three and five often play in ways that suggest they are not ready to give up the option of being both sexes, with little girls trying to urinate standing up and boys walking round with pillows under their T-shirts feigning pregnancy. Given that it means relinquishing one half of human experience it is easy to see that we might regard it as a serious loss to our young selves.

Body language

The messages we are give about our bodies often stretch back to the time when we were 'potty trained'. At this time we are conscious of the opinions of those around us who have, more or less, open access to our bodies. By their actions, comments, by their encouragement or censor we come to understand whether our bodies are acceptable, pleasurable, basically good, or dirty, requiring strict discipline, unacceptable, shameful, to be hidden. These messages are engraved on our developing sense of self, becoming an integral part of our view of ourselves as sexual, bodily beings.

~

Marilyn's father would tease his children about their bodies each night in the bath. Perhaps this filled some sadistic or envious need of his own. It left Marilyn with a feeling of contempt for her body which, as she saw it, had left her open to such humiliation. She wanted to diet until her body disappeared and said 'any amount of body is too much body'.

~

Parental access to the bodies of their children raises issues of the appropriateness of boundaries. At what point does enthusiasm or passion for our child become sick rather than healthy? Each child needs to feel attractive, capable of being provocative, in the safety of trusting the adults to respond appropriately.

~

Alice and Mary waited until their thirties before sharing memories of bathtime as infants with their father. He used the opportunity to 'explore' their bodies, telling them that they were his 'beautiful daughters' and that he was 'checking their development because he was so proud of them'. As children they had never discussed these experiences, although both felt uncomfortable about them, aware that such behaviour did not feel normal, but too young to be sure of the facts or summon help. Both women had experienced sexual difficulties in their relationships with men because they felt likely to be exposed or humiliated by them.

~

Oedipal relationships

As the child grows, he or she becomes more aware of their genital sexuality and its role in relationships. Competition, usually with the parent of the same sex, is a consequence of this growing awareness. The child 'falls in love' with the parent of the opposite sex, wanting to have them for themselves and no longer have to share them with the other parent. In their fantasy world the other parent is beaten, vanquished, even destroyed, leaving them, happily ever after, with the parent-object of their choice.

Such competition leaves the son yearning for his mother and engaged in fantasized battle with his father, and the daughter wanting closeness with father while dismissing mother. These are fantasies, but are often powerfully enacted by children whose prime goal becomes one of separating the parents. If the parents are happy adults with a strong relationship, such 'attacks' by the children can be easily identified and will tend to stir up amusement rather than anxiety. For parents who are themselves still emotionally immature, in relationships that are unhappy or insecure, or who never resolved their own early sexual experiences as children satisfactorily, such infantile attacks lead to a destabilizaiton of the family. Some adults respond to the child as if their fantasy was adult and real, instead of developmental and psychological.

The child is horrified if his or her attack really destroys a parent or their relationship. The horror is even greater if the desired parent acts-out a sexual relationship. Such an acting-out is not associated with either parental or sexual love, but instead is coming out of a mismatch of infantile fantasy and adult instinctual sexual needs, unfettered by responsibility. Thus the child is often left feeling guilty and responsible because it was their own fantasy. In order to conquer the terrifying emotions such encounters cause the child, he or she often develops an elaborate fantasy of a special relationship between themselves and the parents.

~

Katrina was sexually abused by her father from the age of eight. She became increasingly distanced from the rest of the family, and from friends, because she felt 'special' and 'unique' in her relationship with a father who she believed was 'in love' with her. This belief system helped her to survive six years of abuse when she often felt humiliated and hurt but would squash these unacceptable feelings out of sight. She had felt unloved by her mother for as long as she could remember and it never dawned on her to ask for mother's help to save her. In many ways she remained in competition with her mother for her father's attention, and gained a shaky self-esteem based on her belief that she had beaten mother. When she was fourteen she realized, with the shock of an abandoned lover, that her father had turned his attentions to her youngest sister. It was this realization which shattered her precarious defence mechanisms of 'specialness' and left her, a shattered child angrily denouncing the abusing father.

~

The oedipal stage of sexual development, in which the child fantasises about a sexual partnership with a parent, is ridden with both excitement and anxiety. The little girl has to relinquish the close nurturance of the mother to compete with her for father's attentions. Most women stay more intimately connected with their mothers – and generally stay with women rather than men for all aspects of their lives apart from genital sex, suggesting that father rarely seems like a secure enough source of loving to relinquish mother as the primary source. Meanwhile, little boys also fear competition with the much bigger and stronger father, and according to Freud think that father might castrate them in this battle. Men who feel psychologically castrated in adult life usually blame a woman for this state, although it is their own desires for the mother which put them into psychological danger from their father.

Oedipal resolution

The resolution of the Oedipal stage requires a capacity to relinquish hopes of partnership with a parent by identifying with the parent of the same sex, lessening the anxieties and freeing the child's mind for the stresses of more intellectual development. Clearly this can happen best in a home in which love is clearly and strongly expressed between all the members, but with clear demarcation about the appropriateness of intimacy and physical contact, and the parents forming a separate, united decision-making body at some distance to the growing child. This allows for love to become the primary focus of emotional need into which future sexuality can be planted, rather than sexuality being the only driving force around which love may be loosely hung as clothing or disguise.

This resolution is also the stage at which the child's super ego (the internal policing system) becomes most firmly established. In this way it comes to police the relationship between love and sex thereafter, as well as standard-setting for many other areas of activity. The development of the superego seems to be rather different in boys and girls. Morality in women is usually relationship-centred, whereas men are more likely to give ideology a central position in deciding right from wrong. This is a major difference in development, and is presumably at least partly socially ordained because of the view that men and women will be required, as adults, to fulfil differing roles. As roles merge in adulthood to a considerable extent, such differences may also be lessened, but for the time being they often represent a considerable hurdle to men and women understanding or respecting each other's different points of view of morality.

I witnessed a relatively innocent example of this difference at a recent conference. A woman, having plucked up courage for some time, gave voice to her opinion of the subject under discussion. A male colleague, someone who saw himself as her friend, immediately leapt into the debate to correct her pronunciation of a famous poet's name. Many women in the audience felt outraged that he should risk undermining or hurting her in this way. He merely shrugged off such a relationship-centred concern and said that the poet in question was important in his culture and he felt it was his moral imperative to make sure his name was correctly pronounced. Interestingly, the woman concerned then immediately leapt to his defence, making sure that his feelings were not hurt in the fray by the very women who were trying to support her.

Because the superego is most strengthened around the

time that infantile sexuality is being controlled and resolved, much of its structure relates to sexuality generally. The male and female differences are also clear in the sexual arena, so that although it takes both a man and a woman to 'play' heterosexuality, and we might hope that in this game one set of rules should apply, this is still far from the case. Men and women often set different standards of behaviour for themselves within the context of this one relationship. This enables 'good' wives to demonstrate goodness by forgiving erring husbands, who live by different rules to those they set their wives. There is a considerable weakness in any game in which the players accept different rules. In a game as intimate as sexuality, this weakness has mortal dangers for the players.

Adolescence and beyond

Full genital sexuality begins to awaken during adolescence. In many ways this is unfortunate timing, as the individuals are often distracted from any academic pursuits by the insistence of their developing bodies, and are usually not yet able to take full responsibility for their sexuality and its consequences. Despite the fact that historically we have lengthened education and children's dependence on their parents, their bodies (because of better nutrition) are maturing earlier. This makes adolescence ever longer and more difficult to negotiate. Parents often experience their children's developing sexuality as threatening, and try to stamp it out or restrict it as much as possible. This makes the transitional stage even more difficult for the teenager, awash with hormones, egged on by peer advice, filled with romantic hopes and dreams and them imprisoned at home with anxious parents. Perhaps it is not surprising that, for many, first sexual experiences are more likely to be remembered for the anxieties and restricted practicalities rather than great physical enjoyment.

The love attachments of adolescence are notoriously insecure as a basis for sexual exploration. Early experiences can mar future sexuality, although luckily human nature seems remarkably resilient at this stage. Even so, the potential for both emotional and physical harm is great in these early attempts to mix sex and love in reasonable amounts. Few adolescents have a well-developed capacity to take care of themselves or each other, a pathway commonly used by adults as part of loving a sexual partner. Thus, issues of contraception and infection are often avoided rather than discussed; anxiety often kills the ability to be caring and loving.

For most of us, sexuality takes practice if it is to be enjoyable rather than simply functional. Recent generations have set high standards of sexual expectations, and yet a large percentage of people, and particularly women, do not enjoy sex throughout life. Freudian theory held that women needed to develop a passive stance sexually if they were to be perfectly and femininely fulfilled. Such theories were associated with thoughts that vaginal orgasms were in some sense more mature than clitoral ones. Nowadays, advice to women is more likely to underline the need to take an active role in defining their own pleasures, including direct clitoral stimulation.

Arousal and orgasm require a capacity to 'let go' of self-control even if only momentarily. Letting go requires a willingness to be disinhibited and to trust appropriately. It is easiest to trust within the context of loving and being loved. However, passion is easily killed by predictability, stability and boredom, and trust is sensitive to any hint of betrayal. Thus the maintenance of any loving sexual relationship requires the right degree of excitement and safeness. That balance may be different for each partner, adding further complications to the equation. It is probably a reflection of the precariousness of this balance that society tries to order it within a socially acceptable relationship – that of marriage. However, we live in times in which marriage has proved quite unable to contain the instability of the loving sexual relationship.

The need for stability is often quoted as the need for a secure basis in which to rear children. Inside every adult are the remnants of the child, and so adults have some security needs too. Society, as a collection of adults and children, also likes security. Children, as the tremendously vulnerable products of sexuality, have a tendency to focus parental love on themselves, while also consuming much of their mother's sense of libido for months by their physical dependence. Thus, these products of sexual love can also demolish it for periods of time. Marriage may have become less secure because parents are getting less and less help with small children, while at the same time being subject to ever greater social expectations of good parenting. Such expectations may be contradictory to the needs of stabilizing a happy sexualized loving relationship. Thus by focusing on the needs of children we may, socially, be adding to the instability of the parental relationship, which is contradictory to the long-term aims for the child's stability.

A committed loving sexual relationship is the material of most adult dreams. That it is difficult to achieve and maintain is demonstrated by the rarity with which we meet such a relationship.

6

Loving Friends

Early friendship

Friends become important to us early in life, usually during infant and junior school. Suddenly the opinions of our classmates seem more important than those of our family, and we learn to reveal and develop aspects of our personalities which may have been concealed in our relationships at home. We can be different with friends; we are released from the intense emotions of child/parent relationships, with their demands of dependency and control, into friendships in which we can explore ourselves more freely.

Of course friendships also have rules, but these rules do not feel as absolute as those of the family. These early friendships continue in our first experiences of equal relationships with someone of the same age, relationships in which the demands made and the rewards felt have to be in balanced in both persons. In friendship we find a release from the obligations of the family into a relationship in which it is possible to negotiate the 'terms'.

By the time we begin to make friends, the template of our personality is already heavily etched by both nature (our inheritance) and nurture (our developmental experiences). Unlike our beginnings with the family, when we are relatively helpless to define ourselves, the beginning of friendship does allow us to experiment with our developing sense of self. The first friend marks a departure from the total environment of the family in which the child has been emotionally embedded, and gives the possibility of the child sensing new emotional experiences.

Without the restrictions of family law around in these new relationships, children can sometimes seem surprisingly violent, even rather savage with each other. They may be fiercely competitive or easily hurt, one of the gang or a loner. They may already have had the experience of relating to older or younger siblings and transpose these experiences, for better or worse, into the arena of friendships. Or they my be singled out, exposed for the first time to the hurly-burly of peer group relating.

Because of new freedoms, early friendships tend to be short-term and often require adult encouragement and organization. As we explore new ground in relating we all get it wrong easily, hurt others, get hurt ourselves, feel wounded, or ashamed. This leads to a rapid withdrawal of feeling from that relationship, often accompanied by a quick search for a replacement. Loyalties are quickly struck and then lost. At this early stage in learning about friendships, we are beginning to lay down boundaries of what is tolerable. As we mature these boundaries tend to become more flexible, allowing our friends greater transgressions or differences without such immediate and violent rejection. Equally, we learn how to control and modify our own behaviour with friends, so that it falls more easily into acceptable boundaries. These two processes allow friendships to become more stable, a more helping and holding environment for our emotions and our growing understanding of how we fit into the bigger society.

Some may favour being part of a small group or gang, others want to have a single 'best' friend who is experienced in some ways as our personal property. Research suggest that young girls are more likely to want best friends and young boys be happier in larger groupings. The activities that friends chose to share also demonstrate early differences between the sexes, the girls tending to stay in or around home and play cooperative games, while the boys want to explore further and play more competitively. While there is a degree of stereotyping in these descriptions, they still seem to hold true. Perhaps social stereotyping has already occurred by the time we are at a developmental stage to make friends.

There is often a degree of idealization of our early friends, which can extend to include their families, their hobbies and their opinions. It can feel disconcerting as a mother to find your own four-year-old decrying the fact that you do not make as good puddings as Amy's mother while Amy loves nothing better than to be in your house. If the emotional boundaries around a family are very tense and controlling, this phase offers a considerable threat to family integrity and values. This may be particularly true if the family has 'secrets', parental alcoholism, violence, emotional, physical or sexual abuse. If the risks of visiting children seeing things with clear 'outsiders' eyes – or the risks of your own child seeing another, safer and happier world – are too great, then the family may strengthen its hold, restricting the child within its boundaries and denying friendship.

~

Patrick caused concern at his childminder's because he was so distant from the other children of his age. Whatever overtures were made to him, either by the children themselves, or with adult encouragement, Patrick simply backed away and chose to play alone. He seemed a sad child, not happy with his social isolation, and when caught unawares would often be seen gazing at the other children playing games as if he yearned to join in. When one of his carers talked to Patrick's mother, she was struck by how similar the mother's attitudes were to Patrick's. Two days after this talk, Patrick's father withdrew him from the childminder's, after an explosive scene in which the carers were told to mind their own business and not interfere in other people's families. Anyone who has the care of children will recognize this form of family, and worry about the harm it does to the child's developing sense of social relationships, as well as the worry of what is happening at home which requires such secrecy.

Susan and Diana were 'best friends' from the age of seven. Almost inseparable, they worked together at school, played together in the playground and at home, and spent the majority of time together.

They shared secrets, stories, intimacies, their fears and their happiness over the next four years, until Diana's parents moved to a new home some distance away. The parents had been aware of the intensity of this friendship, but they all felt unprepared for the extent of grief which Susan, in particular, experienced at this traumatic separation. In retrospect, they all felt that they might have 'watered down' the extreme intensity of this early attachment by encouraging other friends, and also have prepared the children better in advance for the separation.

~

'The gang' can be important as a source of securing a position in the 'world' of childhood, which feels safe and perhaps prestigious. Such gangs often have a hierarchical structure, like grown-up life in miniature. Those who exert less effect on the gang are often those who are most dependent on it, while the leaders can always reconstitute new gangs if they lose faith in the old ones. It may be strange to think about love in the world of childhood friendships, given their instability, and yet children often harbour deeply emotional ties to each other, ties which might be quite different next week but are still intensely experienced today.

Adolescent friendship

During adolescence, friends can exert a powerful influence over the way we make choices for our own lives. Our attachment to one or more important friends at this stage can have an almost desperate quality to it: these are the friendships which provide a protective screen between us and the already threatening wider-world. These are the relationships which hold our inadequacies, about sexual exploits and about new emotional experiences. We are probably more vulnerable to the opinions of important others in our lives at this point than at any time in the future. The breakup of a friendship can be at least as painful as the breakup of an early romance. We may well contort our own sense of right and wrong to fit in more closely with our peer grouping, whatever their values and however much these values are at odds with what we have previously learnt. During this stage we are transferring the dependency we have felt for parents onto friends as a stepping-stone towards achieving greater independence in the long term.

~

Nicki's parents were outraged to discover she had been shoplifting with friends; Jon's parents to discover he had sniffed glue; Laura's at her new hairstyle; Peter's at his lack of commitment to school work. But Nicki, Jon, Laura and Peter had all acted with friends in ways which probably surprised them as much at is shocked their parents. Having 'street credibility' is a very important source of self-esteem at this age, and it is established within the norms of our friends. It is interesting that as we try to break free from the conventions of the family, most of us immediately settle for those of friendship instead. However, this is a transitional phase, away from the family, a phase that can, as long as no lasting damage is done, be quickly dismissed once we have a greater sense of self and direction in life.

~

Adult friendship

Towards late adolescence we begin to see ourselves and our friends as more separate beings who can do things differently, have different belief systems, behave in ways we may not always like – and still remain friends. Often the friendships forged at this stage of early independence are some of the most longlasting and important ones in life. The commitment we make to friends is unlike other love attachments. There are no socialized rules to conducting friendships, no formal ceremonies, no promises, few social expectations. This can make friendships uniquely flexible, and yet also vulnerable to taking second or third place amongst other more legitimized relationships.

~

Stuart and Colin met at university, played football and hockey together, shared the ups and downs of early romances, drank together, lived in the same flat for a while, studied for exams, passed and failed together. During the early days of their careers, both were too busy to give much time to their friendship. They were also somewhat competitive. Because of this, their friendship became frozen in their past experiences, they had put it 'on hold'. In their late twenties they remained in touch, however, coming to each other's weddings, having meals with new wives present, all four now feeling a little uneasy.

Stuart heard about Colin's car crash on their friendship 'grapevine' several days after the event. For a moment he even wondered whether they were still close enough for him to visit the hospital. He went nevertheless, and experienced what he later described as the 'thud' of friendship returning. Although not seriously injured, Stuart was in hospital on traction for six weeks. His wife had been more seriously injured in the crash, and in fact died three weeks later. This trauma re-established their friendship, and enabled Stuart's wife, Sally-Anne, to become incorporated within it.

~

Sadly, it is often at the very traumatic moments in life that we come to understand the value of ongoing friendship. We should never be too busy to enjoy good times with friends. This is like putting emotional money into the bank to draw on in the face of life's inevitable tragedies.

Those other, more formalized relationships – with relatives, with lovers, parents, spouses and children – intrude into the space for friendship. Because these other relationships have intense starting times, when lovers or parents and new children are engrossed in each other, friendships can get lost in a haze of hurt feelings of betrayal and abandonment. Some effort is needed to stay in touch with friends as your circle of life widens in relationships, careers and in geographical terms. Unlike other relationships, which have some form of social cement to hold them together, friends have to be actively held together just because both people are interested in one another, care and want to be in each other's lives.

Friends vs lovers and family

Friendship can often seem in competition with other relationships in life, even embattled against them. This seems true whether the friendship is same—sex or between man and woman. Friendships may be forged in the post-sexual phase of a relationship, or there may exist the slightly unsteady pre-sexual phase that will never be consummated. Some friendships have no element of sexuality in them, others have a strong thread of sexual attraction woven into their fabric. Love in friendship may as easily be expressed by avoiding sex as by consummating it. Friendship love also needs to know when it is time to back off a little, get on with family life and let your friends do the same. This may be particularly true when friends have small babies and often seem distant because of their preoccupation with the infant. Children, with their great need to interrupt their parents' relationships with others in order to keep attention for themselves, can represent quite a threat to adult friendships.

Jane, who had no children of her own, found herself increasingly resenting the intrusions of all her friend's babies on her conversation with them. For a while she retreated into friendships with other child-free adults, but missed the contact of several close women friends. Slowly she began to re-explore those friendships, and discovered that, five years on, the deep preoccupation between mothers and children which had excluded her, had now changed, allowing her adult contact with the friends she had missed. Having a first child when she was thirty-eight, she warned these same friends about these changes, thus ensuring that they were not pushed away from her.

~

Perhaps it is a tribute to the strength of love in friendship that it survives these developmental challenges, and reasserts it importance as an emotional safety network from the mid-years onwards. Friendships do seem to represent different things to men and women. Men often congregate in friendship groups which involve activities, usually competitive, which enable them to avoid speaking to each other much. Men friends often know little about each other's emotional experience of life, being more likely to discuss non-personal subjects instead. Women are more likely to see talking as the major activity of their friendship, and to know the other person's emotional ups and downs intimately, sometimes more intimately than spouses or families. Again, these may seem like stereotypes, but they do seem to hold true to a remarkable degree.

Friends may be even more important in societies moving away from the culture of extended families. The roles of uncles, aunts and cousins in the past may now belong to friends. They provide a loving buffer between us and the world, through which we can process our experience of ourselves and of life. Their experience can parallel ours, their preoccupations at any particular life-stage may be similar. They also act as storehouses of memories of past shared experiences. They remember where we have come from as well as meeting us now. This gives them a perspective on the whole process of life rather than this snapshot moment.

People often make a further 'wave' of friends as children mature and leave home. These friendships help to widen our horizons beyond the family, and expand our hobbies and occupations away from home and work. They represent a refreshing new pool in which we can see ourselves mirrored, and come to understand some of the ways that the intervening years have changed us.

The love we experience in friendship is often of a warm, non-intrusive form. We may not take our friends for granted in quite the same way as our spouses, but then we probably worry about them differently too. The intensity of love may only be felt in moments of crisis or great joy and success. The love of friends may be the most altruistic love of our lives, an investment without any certainty of gain. But this love may also take us to the places we remember with most pleasure, and per-suade us to heights of experience our families might have sought to protect us from. Many of us would say we have done both the best and the most foolish things of our lives in the company of friends, swept along with friendship love.

Like all loves, friendship love has to grow and change if it is to survive. It also has times of coldness, irritation, despair. It would be a boring life if we were always in agreement with the friends we love, but it can be deeply hurtful to find that there are areas of ourselves which they do not approve of, dislike, or even condemn. Similarly, it is hard suddenly to see an aspect of an old friend more clearly than before. While your loyalties may remain with them, you can suddenly find your sympathies elsewhere. Friendship love is not always absolutely truthful, but rather will learn to time its honesty in understanding of the other. There are always aspects of the other's life and relationships which should probably forego comment unless asked, and even then only be offered with care! To love a friend does not imply knowing what is right for them. Love often has to stand aside and let events unfurl.

Many would eventually count the friends they love as the most rewarding aspect of their interpersonal relationships, outstripping the intimacy with sexual partners, spouses or children. This is probably because we allow ourselves a wider range of friends and can take what we need from each, give back what they like in us without any expectation that this is the relationship in which everything will be found. Our expectations of friendship may well be more generous than our expectations of other relationships, so they disillusion us least. However, the friendships which do fail or betray often deliver cuts which are hard to forget, perhaps impossible to forgive. The most important aspect of a friendship is to be there when needed, and to be accepting of the other. These are high ideals, but make friendship love very special for many throughout their lives.

7

Love and Hate

Ambivalence

Ambivalence is the simultaneous experience of contradictory emotions or attitudes in our relationship with a single object or person. It is an important aspect of our emotional lives and, at its most extreme, allows us to experience love and hate of the same person. However, it requires that we have considerable emotional maturity and stability in the way we view ourselves in order that these diametrically opposed emotions can coexist. More usually, we experience them alternately, as a rapid flipping of the coin from one side to the other. It is important to understand that they make up the complete coin. Love and hate are not opposites, but part of a whole. The true opposite of love is often held to be indifference.

Originally described as having three components, ambivalence was seen as being present in the conscious mind as an ambivalence of will power: the wish both to do something and not do it at the same time. Many feel this way about taking exercise, for instance. In our intellectual mind, ambivalence allows us to hold opinions which are contradictory to each other, and in our emotions ambivalence allows us to feel powerful and contradictory emotions about the same relationship.

~

When John discovered that Felicity was having an affair he felt a wave of hatred wash over him, more intense than any emotion he had previously experienced. For weeks they lived in a hateful silence interrupted only by arguments. Over the following months they began to rebuild their relationship, making new promises to each other. During this phase, John was surprised to find that he would change between loving and hating Felicity suddenly for very little external reason. He was also surprised to find that this shifting of extreme emotions made him feel physically aroused by her in a way that was very different to their previous romantic sexuality.

Felicity also felt swings of emotion for John. In the early days of their love she had often felt undervalued by him because of the controlled and measured way he expressed his feelings. To some extent it was the fact that she felt he withheld love from her that had driven her to seek more passionate feedback from someone else. She was shocked initially by the power of John's hatred, but also intrigued because she had, at last, produced a powerful response from him. She realized that John had idealized her from the start of their relationship. This had set her up on an emotional pedestal where he admired her and she felt untouched. Idealization had distanced them, making their expressed love lukewarm. By leaping off her pedestal, Felicity had broken the spell that idealization had cast on their love.

Melanie Klein, a psychoanalyst working during the 1920s and 1930s, described ambivalence as the central and earliest experience of our emotional lives, when even as small babies we are aware that our mother is perfectly loving and destructively hateful at the same time. Because this experience is unbearable for a totally dependent and helpless infant, the baby 'splits' the good loving mother from the bad hating mother, believing the two to be separate entities. The good mother can then be loved and adored and the bad mother hated, and in the baby's fantasy world, attacked.

These early experiences have important consequences for our experiences of love and hate in later life. Emotionally, many never manage to 'stick together' these dual aspects of intense intimate relating again, and therefore have to continue to idealize the good and denigrate the bad by a process of splitting and projection. This allows us to push away aspects which do not fit in with our belief system onto people, objects, even nations. As we experience ambivalence first and most intensely with our mother, so this split of good and bad remains associated most extremely in our relationship with women, whether we are male or female. In female development, however, many aspects of the early relationship with mother are transferred onto men later.

~

Nicki's mother was depressed for several years after Nicki's birth. Because of this she had grown-up feeling responsible for her mother's distress and always placated and reassured her mother. This meant that she had to learn to contain her more destructive and violent feelings from her earliest moments, and would turn these against herself, by feeling unworthy, bad, even contemptuous about her value to others. As she matured, Nicki became a charming and popular young woman. Each time a man fell in love with her she would go through a phase of being the 'perfect' companion, bending to the wishes, beliefs and hobbies of the man and apparently enjoying herself by submerging her life into his. Part of this 'submergence' required that his emotions became paramount in their relationship. Her own feelings sunk deep down and for a while, out of sight. However, after several months Nicki would begin to feel unhappy about herself, become convinced that she did not deserve her lover, and would start to 'attack' herself by gaining weight, changing hairstyles and making snide comments about herself. The men soon became alarmed by these changes and departed for other loves.

At this point Nicki felt alone and frightened, and would revert back to the pleasing woman and start the cycle again. At her twenty-eighth birthday party, she was bemoaning the loss of yet another man when her sister confronted her with the question 'Have you ever loved any of them?' This took Nicki aback. One of her basic assumptions about herself was that she had to try hard to be good and loving at all times. She felt transparent, as if her sister's question had suddenly revealed the hateful and bitter aspects of herself which she had tried so hard to hide. For several weeks Nicki felt suicidal, and the intensity of these feelings led her to seek help from a women's group.

She became part of a group which met each week, and gained the support she needed to explore herself more openly and with less fear and negative judgements. For the first time she began to see that there were times when it was possible to feel angry and hateful about someone else, without destroying them and without having to be responsible for the feelings of the other in preference to being responsible to herself. She also began to see that her difficulties in relationships stemmed from her early days learning to relate to her mother, but throughout adult life she had transferred these difficulties into all her relationships with men. Eventually she had to let go of her omnipotent belief that she could manipulate the feelings of those around her into perfect happiness by moulding herself into whatever they wanted. This left her more free to begin to question what she wanted and needed from a partner.

~

Good Women

The early developmental process of splitting good from bad is a universal psychological experience. Because we experience it first in relation to our mothers, our belief in 'good' and 'bad' women being separate breeds is a more deeply held belief than that of 'good' and 'bad' men. Society seeks to concretize these psychological parameters. Social rules have, until recently, been almost exclusively defined by men because of their socioeconomic powers, and therefore women are still subjected to a much more powerful set of 'good' and 'bad' definitions of the self. Such definitions often contaminate love relationships between men and women.

～

Mary was obsessional about housework and yet, one day, put the plug in the kitchen sink and proceeded to flood the kitchen. James was amazed when he returned to find chaos in their previously perfect house. His love for Mary was firmly embedded within his definitions of a 'good woman'. One parameter of goodness was perfect housework done each day to standards which satisfied him. Mary had worked hard for ten years to satisfy him as she too believed that this proved her to be a 'good woman'. Finally something had snapped and she rebelled, from both James's and her own belief systems.

～

Although an extreme example, this couple demonstrate what is still held dear in the majority of households within our culture. Namely that a good woman does the housework and a man who refuses to help is not held to be bad. I still have vivid memories of the state of several of the flats which my male medical student colleagues shared, dirty washing everywhere, unwashed milk bottles and forgotten washing up in sinks, no hoover, no clean bed linen, revolting towels and no toilet paper! 'Boys will be boys' was the attitude they met from cleaners, girl-friends and mothers. Any woman living like that would certainly have attracted harsh, judgemental responses. Those judgements would have been seen to belong to her entire self, for example she would have been called a 'slut', which would have inferred judgement on her sexuality as well as her housework standards.

'Good women' are defined in many ways, all of which seek to make them more amenable as companions, helpmates and support systems to male lovers, friends and colleagues. Until the 1960s, one important parameter of female 'goodness' was the notion of virginity, 'saving herself', having only one sexual relationship in life with her husband – and not being expected to enjoy that too much either. That these concepts were based in the male fantasy of virgin mothers, and never did accurately describe women's experiences of sexuality, made no difference to the vehemence with which society enforced them.

However, society began to change the rules during the 1960s. Why or how this change came about is a matter of dispute. Was it that sexually-aware women now had access to a guaranteed form of contraception, the pill, which relieved anxiety and released them from guilt? This seems unlikely, as each of us knew of women for whom the pill had 'failed' and we were therefore less reassured by its certainty than science would have had us believe. Certainly, although the morality of the men in the 1960s generation shifted rapidly to accommodate women as more willing sexual partners, society's morality shifted more slowly, with its 'bad' judgements always still resting with the women. Even in the early 1970s, women still had to call themselves 'Mrs' to get help at family planning clinics. However, something about the climate of the 1960s allowed individuals who wished to do so to burst through social restrictions, and many women used that window of opportunity to redefine sexual normality for women within our culture. I have often wondered whether there was an impact on the women of that 1960s generation from their mothers' experiences during World War Two. Perhaps their internalized belief systems had been changed by their mothers' snatched freedom in the absence of many of their menfolk during the war, a freedom which that generation rapidly relinquished for themselves in the face of 'victory', but maybe harboured as a hope for their daughters. Thus primed, the daughters of the 1960s grabbed their chance.

Thirty years on, it is possible to reflect on how much and yet also how little society's judgements of 'good' and 'bad' women have shifted, with regard to their sexuality. Princesses may still have to be virgins, but Duchesses are now allowed to have had previous relationships. Living together is now rarely described as 'living in sin', marriage may no longer be seen as 'making an honest woman' of the bride. But do we truly now use the same standards of sexual behaviour to rate men and women, or is there still a shadow of past definitions which cloud our views and responses?

Although several generations of women have fought against these notions, the fact that they originate from our earliest psychological experiences make them hard to attack, and means that they are reinstated with every new generation. This does not make them any more real than they ever were, of course, but extraordinarily powerful within each person's psyche. The concept of living together may be the attempt of the younger generations to find a relationship format which allows them escape from these early established experiences. The reason that many of these relationships break down after marriage may be because earlier notions become psychologically re-established in the minds of one or both partners as soon as they re-enter the original family structure.

~

Deborah had lived with Jim for six years before they married. Theirs was a well-balanced relationship, and both felt that they had defined a way of living together which suited them well. Within weeks of marriage, they started to have arguments over responsibilities and roles which had never caused any rifts in their relationship before. Jim, in particular, wanted Deborah to be different now that she was his wife. Although intellectually he still wanted her to work and be successful, emotionally he now felt that her primary role was with him. Deborah also felt a change in her expectations of Jim, which made her wish that he earned as much money as she did. They had accepted each other prior to marriage in a way which embraced each other as they actually were. Within marriage notions of 'right' and 'wrong' ways of relating reared their head which were at odds with the balance they had defined. Deborah felt increasingly that their relationship was hard work, and wondered where all the fun they had shared had disappeared to. Jim felt challenged and frustrated over his role. Their sexual relationship, once so comfortable, ceased, and they eventually separated.

Talking over their experience several years later, Jim acknowledged that he wanted Deborah to conform to his ideas of 'a good woman' once she was his wife. These ideas were contradictory to the aspects of Deborah he had fallen in love with, and also rather idealistic. Deborah had sensed that Jim was starting to relate to her in this judgemental way, and had also retreated into wanting him to adopt a 'provider' role rather than risk relating intimately and truthfully any longer.

~

Good enough parents

The baby first notices that good and bad mothers are not separate entities in the middle of the first year of life. This is a gradual dawning of awareness, so that the baby is not overwhelmed with anxiety. For such an awareness to develop, a mother must be able to represent a stable self to the baby, both when she is meeting the demands and when she is frustrating them. For the mothers, it is difficult to find such a stability of self in the early days of mothering because the baby's projections, with their absolute belief in goodness and badness, are experienced as overwhelming. Mothers are also immersed in a world in which many maintain the infantile beliefs of the baby about good and bad mothers. Many adults have little or no concept of what a 'good enough' mother might be. We continue, as adults, to remain highly critical of women as mothers throughout their children's lives.

~

Pamela worried about her style of mothering and demanded reassurance from her husband and family on a daily basis. She believed that a good mother would always know what the crying baby wanted, would always predict needs and dangers, and would create a perfect harmony in the mother/child relationship. Anything less than this and she saw herself as a dismal failure. Not surprisingly, in view of these standards, she was failing every day. No amount of reassurance could help her, until she began to have a less extreme vision of being a loving mother. Eventually a health visitor told her that it was important for mothers to fail sometimes, and that the image of the perfect mother she was struggling to be was a fantasy projected from the baby onto herself. When she tried to be less judgemental about herself and more relaxed in the way she reacted to the baby, the health visitor did her best to be supportive. She was interested to note how quickly the husband and family switched from reassurance to criticism, however, and soon realized that Pamela had only managed to maintain her idealistic views on mothering because she was surrounded by a family system which shared similar views.

~

A mother therefore needs an especially strong sense of self, and to be surrounded by others who support this view of her basic 'good enoughness', in order to provide both nurture and frustration in bearable quantities to the growing child. This capacity to tolerate the emotional onslaught from the infant (sometimes combined with that of society), while thwarting the immediate gratification of their needs, requires that the mother can bear ambivalence in her emotional world. If an infant's basic needs for love and nurture are reasonably met, he or she should be able to withstand increasing amounts of frustration. This experience allows the infant to experience the good and bad mother as one person.

As the infant struggles to make sense of this new discovery, he or she will experience rapid swings of mood. Children are often experienced as temperamental at this stage, and many adults maintain this emotional structure into later life. In healthy development, however, it is a stepping-stone to a realization that those we love and depend on are far from perfect, that sometimes we do not like those we love.

Throughout infancy and childhood, the growing child struggles with his or her view of the perfection of the mother and father. In healthy development, this perfection fades to be replaced by a more reasonable assessment of parents' strengths and weaknesses. We are often left with the remnants of our belief in perfection, however. We like to make our mothers omnipotent, and our fathers divine, in order to continue to believe in our hopes that someone can save us from the anxieties of life. It is much easier for a child to believe that a parent is either good or bad than to bear the knowledge that both are flawed. Often the child splits the good into one parent and the bad into the other, in order to hold the intolerable ambiguity more easily.

~

Pamela grew up believing that her father was perfect: she saw him as a wise, dependable and deeply religious man, in whom she trusted for both guidance and admiration. Meanwhile, she perceived her mother as a bitter and unpleasant woman with little time for others, interested only in herself. On the death of her father, she discovered from his documents that he had lived a double life, his sexual and emotional energies being channelled towards men. Rather than rethink her vision of her father, she extended her dislike of her mother, making her coldness responsible for the father's behaviour. At her mother's funeral she met an aunt, her mother's sister. This sister shared with her the memory of a happy and sunny young woman who seemed destined for great things. Pamela could not believe that this young woman had been her mother and that marriage to her father had been a crucial factor in the destruction of a mother she could have loved.

~

For Pamela, this discovery came too late to change her relationships with either parent onto a more honest footing. Most of us achieve a gradual resolution of the split of good and bad, and by our thirties can see parents more accurately.

Alongside this development, the infant cannot forget the attacks and rage that he or she has focused on the bad mother, believing her to be safely distant from the good mother. Fearing that the good mother may also have been damaged, the infant feels a sense of guilt and a desire to make amends, to make reparation. Guilt and the desire to make amends thereby become part of our coping ability when faced with future ambivalence. We can be safe to love and hate in intimate relationships if we are confident that both ourselves and our partners can eventually acknowledge and make repairs for their more hateful words and actions.

~

Susan and Peter had always been seen as a perfect couple and happy family in the village in which they lived. Peter had an intense love of both Susan and the children, which made him possessive and meant that the family was relatively isolated. During his mid-thirties he experienced problems at work and began to resent the stresses he was under by comparison with what he imagined was Susan's much easier life at home. He experienced these changes as a collapse of the world he had built, and saw Susan as increasingly responsible for this, even though she was unaware of any problems. In blaming Susan he was splitting off much of himself – his own depression and sense of inadequacy for instance – and projecting it onto her. One night, unable to bear the tension any longer, he killed Susan and the children as they slept. As soon as he saw Susan dead, however, all his projections seem to return to him like poisonous arrows and in blind despair he killed himself too.

~

Dependence vs independence

The love/hate ambivalence is only the first of many ambivalent emotions with which we have to learn to grapple in order to establish and maintain close relationships. Another important aspect of ambivalence centres on feelings of dependence and independence. Most of us require a relationship in which we can maintain some safe dependence without risk of humiliation or shame. The greater the stress, the more difficult the life events, the more we may experience that desire for dependence. However, we all feel an equally powerful tug towards independence, control of our own destiny, personal freedom. Often, adult relationships are seen as opening possibilities for one or other of these states, rather than being selected because they can offer the needed combination of the two. This may lead one partner to express dependence, while the other expresses their joint need for freedom. Like many attempted solutions to ambivalent emotions, this can never represent a very stable state of affairs. It only takes one partner to get an inkling of the other side of their own emotional experience for the relationship to fail, or to see-saw dramatically as partners change roles.

~

Petula, married when only seventeen, went straight from her parents' home to her new relationship. She had therefore never had a moment in which her life belonged to her, but lived instead to please others. By being pleasing she managed to enmesh the others, her husband and parents, into looking after all her dependency needs. Until she was thirty-five this state of affairs suited all involved. Petula was an only child, and her parents enjoyed, even lived for, the role they played in her life. Her husband, David, liked the role of family leader and liked to believe that he was independent of any need to lean on others: he believed that Petula was the dependent one. However, as their two children reached adolescence Petula began to feel uneasy about the limitations which were placed on her life. She envied her daughter's freedom for further study, and enrolled herself into the Open University, even though David had cautioned against it. During her first week of summer school, Petula realized that she had grown up a great deal since her own adolescence, and now enjoyed freedoms which would have frightened her eighteen years earlier. Returning home, Petula was determined to make some changes to her life, which she increasingly saw as a prison rather than a secure place.

Meanwhile, David knew that these changes made him feel insecure. He blamed Petula for his uncomfortable anxieties, and reminded her that he had never wanted her to join the OU in the first place, because he had known that it would be disruptive. Although she was happy moving towards a more equal balance within herself of dependence and independence, David was resistant to acknowledging that this change had revealed his own insecurities.

~

Love and idealism

Some people think that they are capable of experiencing a 'pure' form of love, uncontaminated by extreme feelings of rage and hate. This may be a reflection of a universal split between idealism and realism. The idealist is more likely to experience love of things and places, love of God or love of a distant person. This allows them to maintain love unsullied at a few paces removed and often experienced as a spiritual emotion. The realist is more likely to view love as an earthy part of natural experience with other people, and equate it easily with sexuality. In addition, the ideal form of love often requires that the lover merges with the loved object as if they were one, while realism may allow for a form of partnership love, but would not risk submerging the self in the other.

Love of another adult requires that we give them an additional value over and above that which we might accord them in friendship. We bestow this gift towards the person or people who strike deep into our inner worlds and touch some aspect of our emotional life. Thus we do not bestow love randomly, loving the first person we set eyes on when we next wake up (as the fairy queen is made to do in *Midsummer Night's Dream*), but instead make a highly personal choice based on our own inner needs. The gift of love then secures this person both as an emotional bond to hold them close and as a means of our being able to hold them as our choice over other possibilities. This can be a one-way or two-way process. In almost all relationships it is more strongly felt and maintained in one direction than the other.

In a sense, we construct this love, and the notion of 'working at marriage' is probably a description of how that construction needs regular maintenance without which it can easily crumble. The construction is not concrete and static but dynamic, and has to have the strength and flexibility to allow life events to impinge on it without irreversible damage. When a part of our love construction is chipped we feel pain and anxiety. Such experiences may make us rush to mend it rather like we might hasten to a dentist if we chipped a tooth. However, many people respond to pain and anxiety with anger and rage. 'How dare the person I love hurt me like this?' Thus a small chip in the love construction may lead on to argument, rage, despair and a desperate power struggle, rather than reparation. At this moment the gift of love we bestowed becomes vulnerable and can easily flip over into hating. Because we have given the person we love a special value above others, the extent of that hate can be much greater than anything experienced elsewhere.

Many couples describe a process in which the very aspect of their partner they originally loved most becomes exactly the aspect they come to hate and detest. This suggests that our power to give additional value is equal and opposite to our power, when hurt, to subtract it. We regress at these moments, driven by the anxiety, pain and anger to feel and behave in a more childlike way. However we resolved the early love/hate split in childhood, it will now reappear. If we have maintained inner beliefs of perfect love, then this new discovery of its opposite will be a brutal blow to our understanding of relationships, and we can feel deeply betrayed. In our hate it is more likely that we will experience ourselves as betrayed by the person we loved rather than betrayed by the ideal of love. We hate the person rather than the experience of love/hate. The contradiction of both emotions feels more painful than allowing ourselves just to hate. However, if we cannot resolve this experience of betrayal in a way that allows us to understand ourselves and our attitudes to love/hate better, we are in great danger of falling into the next relationship with the same flawed expectations, and thus risking further experiences of betrayal which will hurt us but not increase our understanding.

Many of an individual's vulnerabilities, wishes and desires remain hidden in daily life. Hiding parts of ourselves allows us to remain, to some extent, opaque and therefore able to construct a 'social self' we feel happy about exposing. In intimate relationships that 'social self' is gradually replaced by a more honest sharing of our fears, vulnerabilities, weaknesses and flaws. In this way, loving partners often know a very different 'self' in the other person than their friends and colleagues do. Love provides the stable and trusting context in which such sharing is possible. However, it also means that we are more exposed and vulnerable in those relationships than in others. In relating in this way we presume that our partner will be able to cope psychologically both with exposing their own vulnerabilities and accepting ours.

In relationships which are poised between loving and hating, such exposure represents considerable risks for the partners involved. What is exposed during the loving phase may be used against the partner, to their shame and humiliation, in the hating phase. It is only in those relationships stable enough to contain the loving/hating dichotomy of feelings without collapse that intimate sharing is truly a safe endeavour.

Not only can a partner expose another in a public way when they have shared previously hidden parts of the self, they may also be able to have a strong influence on that partner's sense of self. All exposure is met by some form of feedback. If the feedback is positive and confirms the person as valuable, then a 'feeding' intimacy is established in which the partner grows in confidence and self-esteem. If the feedback is negative and hostile, the partner's sense of self will suffer with lessening self-esteem and decreasing confidence. While this is a painful situation for one partner, they might feel they have already exposed too much to break off the relationship, and instead continue being sucked further into a decline of their sense of self. Meanwhile the other partner may feel powerful and good by comparison and therefore their self-esteem and confidence will grow. In this way relationships with gross inequalities of emotional power are established. The love/hate ambivalence has been converted into a good/bad split reminiscent of the baby's early split in his or her perception of mother. One partner holds the 'good' elements and the other the 'bad'. If the supposedly 'bad' partner attempts to rebel and re-establish themselves as worthwhile and valuable, the 'good' partner may well become depressed, uncertain of their own worth.

~

Gertrude had always wondered why Kevin stayed with her. She saw herself as unattractive and difficult to live with. He was so kind that she frequently thought of him as saintly. Kevin shared these thoughts, thinking that he was, indeed, a kind person to put up with the impossible Gertrude. In the circumstances it puzzled both of these partners that it should be Gertrude who regularly experienced depressions, while Kevin seemed to breeze through life in harmony with himself. At a Christmas party for Kevin's company, Gertrude met several people who told her of a very different

Kevin, one who could be short-tempered and indifferent with his staff. This was unexpected and made Gertrude look differently at Kevin's behaviour. She began to see that much she had previously considered saintly was really intensely annoying. In her mind she began to argue with him and call him names like 'goodie goodie two shoes' and then feel bad about herself for having such thoughts.

If she dared to challenge any of his helping behaviour, Kevin would chastise her for being difficult to please. 'But,' she thought, 'a lot of what he does and says doesn't please me. He does it to please himself.' The more her thoughts dragged her in the direction of criticism, the more unreasonable Kevin saw her as being. Eventually Gertrude suggested that they go to Relate and see a marriage counsellor. Sure that a counsellor would share his views, Kevin went willingly and took up much of the session expounding his views of their problems. At the end of the session the counsellor told Kevin that he would like to kick him for being so smug, and wondered aloud how Gertrude had tolerated it for so long.

~

Midlife is a time when people tend to take stock of their life experience so far. This usually includes an inner, personal review of relationships as well as careers and friendships. It is a time at which our own individual mortality becomes more real and therefore life seems to become more urgent. Situations we have suffered for years suddenly become unendurable and changes, often drastic changes, are made. It is also a time in life when wide swings of mood may have mellowed, when ambivalence becomes easier to bear, even in our closest relationships, and when companionship may become more important than passion. At this time the ambivalence of the external world may become more evident. Splits that previously seemed comprehensible may now look decidedly stupid. At the far ends of many spectrums, good and bad do exist, but the expanse of those spectrums becomes increasingly apparent as our own capacity for ambivalence grows. It is this process which allows us to become more tolerant and less judgemental as time goes by.

Perhaps the greatest test of this new found midlife tolerance comes in the shape of adolescent children. During adolescence children test parents' capacity to love greatly as they experiment with their own personalities. While exercising new freedoms, their capacity for also exercising responsibility often develops more slowly. At one moment grown-up and demanding respect of an adult, at another feeling vulnerable, stressed and wanting to be rescued by parents, the adolescent moves backwards and forwards in an uneven path towards true maturity. Parents who have loved their children with remarkably little ambivalence through childhood now find themselves hating these outsized children in their home. The battles between parent and teenager are important; the emerging adult can begin to define themselves in the safety of a loving and relatively secure relationship, before the traumas of the unknown world outside of the family. However, parents need to have come to terms with their own strengths and weaknesses, and those of the parental relationship, if they are to hope to deal with the ambivalent feelings between parents and children at this stage.

Ambivalence means that our capacity for loving has a flaw, a weak spot. The stronger the love the more that flaw can become exposed. Other emotions — envy, jealousy, pride, shame, anger and anxiety — can slide into the crack, breaking apart the whole coin of love and hate that we started with, distorting it, leaving it condemned.

8

Object Love

Love is not primarily a relationship to a specific person: it is an attitude, an ordination of character which defines the relatedness of the person to the world as a whole.

ERIC FROMM

At what point in our lives do we expand our vision of loving from the personal relationship to wider horizons, to objects, places and ideologies? Does this represent a new-found maturity, or an escape from the commitment of the personal?

A new-born infant is not interested in the world around him or her. Even if born in the Tate Gallery there is no masterpiece brilliant enough to focus those eyes and demand an emotional response! And yet soon, within a few weeks, the baby can focus on, and become fascinated by, facial characteristics – a smiling mouth for instance – and by movement, colour and sound. The capacity to be distracted by and entranced by new external experiences grows with the baby, partly in response to his or her own internal needs, and partly as a response to the world around then. This world is explored with fingers, mouth, eyes, ears and nose. Most babies want to experiment with new objects, sucking and chewing them as well as gazing at them or listening for them.

At the same time, infants are exploring their own peripheries, their fingertips and later their toes, as if they were mapping-out their own physical boundaries in relationship to everything else around them. Sooner or later, once they have reached their toes, they want to get up and become mobile in order to further their exploration. From then on, every step, every button, every object, whether it is a steep staircase, Mum's stereo or a plug socket, becomes the non-specific object of their attention. With no regard to safety, each and every object is subjected to scrutiny simply because it is new. During the course of this explorative phase some objects come to be more familiar and more pleasing to the growing child than others. Some retain the attention while others are discarded; gradually children become selective in their choice of objects and some things please more than others. Perhaps some comfort, some excite and some just fascinate. One child may choose a classical teddy bear to cuddle for security, another may want a blanket or a handkerchief. To some extent they may choose what is available, but having picked and conferred specialness on their object of choice they then remain attached to that object for some time – months and sometimes years. They will not want replacements or something much the same, it is the one object to which they have become attached and to which they give their developing capacity for love.

This object has been called a transitional object because it helps the child make the transition from an intense attachment to another person to relating to a wider range of experiences. Such transitional objects ease the child's anxieties about separation or loss of the loved person. We learn at a young age that objects can comfort us, console us and protect us from some of the anxieties connected with relationships with other people.

This learning is translated throughout our emotional and intellectual development, until as adults we can use our capacity for love objects and of the world around us, as well as with people. In order to do this we need to develop processes by which we can 'take in' this world as an experience and then understand and appreciate it. Jean Piaget, a child psychologist, described two processes by which we achieve these aims. Assimilation is the absorption of an experience, taken in whole and understood within the limits of that person's present limitations. Accommodation is the taking in of an experience in such a way that our present limits are expanded to allow us to understand something new. Thus the child moves from being something of a spectator of experiences, towards a more interactive approach to the world. This interaction allows for a feedback loop between the baby and the outside so that the baby can influence, to some extent, the objects that he or she is observing.

Feedback loops eventually allow the child to interact with his or her environment with an increasing sense of mastery. The toy which was originally only held as a distraction for a few minutes before tea is now seen differently. It can be used, for instance, to hit your sister on the head, thereby provoking a response, or it can be dipped into your food to act as a tool for distributing the food to a greater area of carpet. Having achieved these aims once, they can be repeated thereafter. The infant has thereby moved from simply being enchanted by the object to experimenting with ways of using it for his or her greater pleasure.

Early in the second year of life an infant will assume that 'out of sight' is not merely 'out of mind' but 'no longer exists'. By closing their eyes or putting hands over their face they can, in imagination, make their families disappear! However, as the second year of life progresses the child gains 'object permanency' and now a mental image of the object remains on the mind of the child, even in its absence. Now the child is motivated to search out something or someone who disappears. This capacity to maintain a mental image is the beginning of our ability to symbolize, and from this our development of language can proceed.

Until the age of six or seven our thought processes are not rational. We know an increasing range of things, but we do not know how we know them. Magical thinking, belief in great powers and a certainty that the self still remains at the centre of all that we see and experience means that this experience can only be distorted. The child is still relying on intuition to understand much of what he or she sees, and his or her version of life is 'impressionistic', rather than a sequence of logically argued steps. Between the age of seven and the end of primary education at eleven a change occurs, as the child's centre of the universe changes from the self to the outside world. Although thought processes are still rather concrete they are now subjected to external validation and argument. The 'magical' powers of the parents lessen, while the need for external rules and structure to life becomes greater.

During adolescence something wonderful happens to the thinking processes of some, although not all, children. Concrete thinking is replaced by a more abstract view of the world. Thinking can now make connections backwards and forwards in time, and between different topics. Ideas and fantasies can be mixed so that the person is capable of having an idea which comes from within without any external experience to stimulate it.

Throughout these phases we are influenced by the people, the culture, the religions and the environment in which we grow. Our personalities interact with all these external possibilities in a way that makes both our experience and what we do with it unique.

Our capacity to enjoy, experiment with and develop in active relationship to our environment can be maximized or minimized by adults within the family or by a wider society. The toddler who has run barefoot on the sand knows something that a child who has had her feet bound can never know. The child raised in the countryside will have different freedoms and different limitations to a child raised in an inner city area. Such experiences affect the way we perceive the world, expanding or limiting our visions. The son encouraged to climb trees and explore will always have a different relationship to his world than his sister if she stays home to play with dolls. If she wants to be out climbing trees then her experience can be more like his, but the weight of advertising, films and cartoons she will have seen will already be creating that experience into 'tomboy' territory and thus making her experience different to her brother's.

During this development we are encouraged to create objects of childhood art. The school rooms we sit in are wallpapered with the end products of this encouragement. Our parents, if kindly, show great pride in our latest masterpiece, albeit two toilet rolls stickyback sellotaped to a cereal packet. In this way our capacity to interact with objects in order to create something new and 'of ourselves' which is then appreciated by others is encouraged. As we begin to take more and more notice of others, so too will we be more interested in what they are producing, these external symbols of each inner world. Our relationship to these products of the growing artist may take many forms. Almost always, alongside love or pride of something beautiful, we find envy, competition, disinterest and destruction. Controlling these other forces so that the child can respect his or her own work in the context of the work of all the others in a class, a year or a generation is the complex task of the sensitive teacher.

Not everyone can be talented at exposing their own inner worlds by external creations but each and every child is capable of learning to appreciate the products of others, more gifted than themselves, as long as they feel valued for and competent in some other sphere of activity. It is hard to respect the loved objects of others unless we can maintain the capacity to love and value our own objects.

This development is driven by a variety of forces: the child's need to master his or her world, to understand it; by the need to calm anxieties both in the personal world of relationships where our anxieties are about loss and separation; and in the outside world where our anxieties are of a more existential nature, such as about the meaning of life and our own mortality; and by our need to sublimate some or all of our sexual energies into other, perhaps safer, fields of activity. It was Freud who first talked about the need to sublimate sexual energies, although he was never very clear about what constituted sublimation and was therefore defensive about what were normal intellectual and creative pursuits.

Freud also pondered on the degree to which someone who pursues creative hobbies or tasks with sublimated sexual energy is a narcissist, that is, someone still enchanted by themselves rather than any external object. Any object they create is loved by the creator because it is perceived as part of him or herself and not as a separate object. From a different perspective Melanie Klein wondered to what degree we engaged in creative tasks in order to repair that part of the first loved object, namely the 'bad' mother, who we had attacked and damaged in our fantasies.

Symbols, myths and dreams

Human beings have a remarkable capacity for symbolism. Objects, ideas and experiences can become imbued with a wide range of emotional meaning. Through the medium of symbolism we can give concrete representation to our inner wishes, ideas and conflicts.

Throughout time and across cultures there is a tendency for the symbols to be shared and understood universally. Sometimes symbols allow us to evoke some idea or belief which would be difficult or impossible to perceive otherwise. For instance, the symbol of a crown evokes notions of royalty more quickly than many words could do. In this way an abstract idea can be made material and instantly recognizable. Sometimes symbols are also concrete however. The sun, for instance has sometimes been used to evoke the concept of a particular royal dynasty too.

In psychoanalytic terms, symbols link the manifest and obvious content of speech, thought or behaviour to the hidden or latent meaning. Dreams are a personal example of this, and myths a cultural example.

The fairytale myth of Cinderella tells of the belief that if as a woman you can be young, pretty and very very good (even in impossible circumstances) then your prince will come and rescue you, loving and protecting you 'happily ever after'. There can be few young women who do not, at times, yearn for such a rescue. Many young men also are attracted to the idea of being the prince who offers salvation. In real life we know, particularly as we get older, that such a scenario is unlikely, and even when acted out can often end in tears rather than lifelong happiness. But, because we continue to wish for a happy ending to grim reality in our inner worlds, the myth holds its spell over us, symbolizing that inner yearning.

I can still remember the murmur of excitement and anxiety that ran around an infant school hall one

Christmas when the little girl acting as Cinderella told her prince, 'No thank you, I want to grow up to be a solicitor!' Symbolism of the inner world collided with the different reality of an outer world and each of the audience was jolted by that collision.

Dreams represent a personal form of symbolism, in which, because we are asleep and our defences are less active, our unconscious world tries to speak to us in a symbolic way. Freud used to think it was possible to attach particular meaning to objects in dreams because they were universal symbols. Thus church spires might be penises, trains entering tunnels intercourse, and the sea the unconscious itself. Usually dreams are more personalized however, and we are each the expert on what our own dreams mean. During analysis it is often helpful to keep an immediate record of dreams with a notebook by the bed, because as we all know they have a habit of fading fast in the memory once we are awake. Dreams often let us express and experience the hidden repressed and more ugly side of love relationships, the angry and murderous bits.

~

Claire often dreamt that she was drowning her children in the swimming pool. This had two connecting meanings for her. One was a safe expression of her hostile feelings that usually remained well hidden in her waking mind, the other was that the water in the pool resembled the unconscious 'soup' in which she felt that she and the children wallowed together, it hardly mattering if they were above or below water. She often had the dream when left together with the children without other adult company for several days, as if that was when she was most threatened both internally and externally by the pressures she felt.

~

Displacement

Thus dreams and myths allow us to displace the extremes of our emotional lives into safe arenas. We can yearn for a perfect and self-saving love and we can experience the murderous, anxiety-provoking aspects of 'the real thing' encapsulated safely in the myth or the dream. The capacity to displace emotional energy from the person we love into symbolic experiences is a sophisticated defence of our loving feelings. By detaching some of the energy and then projecting it into a safe arena we are protecting both our own feelings and those of the person we love. However, the balance between this being a healthy or unhealthy process lies in how much of our emotional energy we feel we have to displace.

If we regularly displace most or all of our energy into 'safe' objects or experiences, we are left with little sense of how we feel towards a person. The vague shadow of an intense emotion may remain to taunt us and confuse us, but the big burst of energy is now attached elsewhere. That 'elsewhere' is sometimes an illness. It is by this process that people convert the unbearable contradictions and confusions of loving relationships into those illnesses which used to be thought of as 'hysterical' phenomena. Now we have a better understanding of the connections between the mind and the body it is easy to see how interlinked they are.

~

Maggie commented on how calm and unconcerned she was about her forthcoming marriage. However, her sister, Annabel pointed out that Maggie's arthritis had flared up again since the decision to go ahead with the wedding. Maggie had to agree that her joints were always more troublesome in the face of important emotional events. Annabel suggested that marrying Jon was not as straightforward a business as Maggie's calm exterior suggested. In fact Jon had recently confessed to several affairs during their three-year relationship, and this revelation had, somehow, led to them agreeing to marry in order to help Jon contain his actions. This conversation led Maggie to feel uneasy and tearful, emotions which she had previously connected with her painful joints. Now she began to wonder if the joints were providing her with an 'alibi' for how distressed she was feeling at a time when she thought she should be happy.

~

Freud called the form of displacement of emotion which Maggie demonstrates 'conversion', because the energy concerned can cross from an external experience into the internal world of the body. In this way the body becomes the object of Maggie's hateful and attacking aspects, while she maintains her positive loving feelings externally for Jon. Sometimes the body can become the love object, as we displace aspects of our sexual satisfaction from the genitals into a safer 'erogenous zone'. Thus in times of sexual repression the sight of a shapely ankle or tight-belted waist was experienced as arousing. Because culture actively encourages young women to be narcissistic about their own bodies, they can easily become their own love objects. Pampering their own bodies can then become a metaphor for sexual satisfaction. Having a beautiful body may be an alternative to having a sexual relationship, because acquiring and maintaining that body takes the displaced sexual energy and excitement away from its original aims.

~

Elena spends up to three hours a day exercising, toning and having beauty treatments. Having trained as a beauty therapist she is an expert on what is available, and is demanding of those who treat her. She describes her favourite occupation as running on the jogging machine. During this time she faces a full-length mirror and experiences herself and her reflection with great satisfaction. In many ways Elena is healthy and happy, and certainly a woman who would catch your eye with her stunning looks. However she came to therapy when her second marriage looked about to fall apart because of her total lack of interest in a sexual relationship. It was immediately evident from her description of each day's activity that her whole attention focused on herself for herself. In some ways this pleased her, even satisfied her, and yet it left her feeling disconnected and unattached to anyone else, including her husband – who she claimed, in a rather unemotional way, to love.

Elena's father had always been a critical and spiteful man, who constantly remarked on the looks of his wife and both daughters. Some of Elena's earliest memories involved gazing into mirrors searching for imperfections which might attract his attention and wondering what she could do about them. For Elena, much sadness and anxiety lay buried in that relationship with her father, and yet she also secretly yearned to be the perfect creature who could hold a man enslaved by her beauty. It was this secret yearning which had directed much of her life, including her choice of career and her choice of husbands, both of whom wanted a beautiful wife. Elena had displaced all the energies which might have been directed towards father as her primary male loved one, and then into future lovers and partners, into her own body instead. This allowed her to feel safe and satisfied and to keep at bay the anxiety about her imperfections and 'unlovability'. It also allowed for her to displace her angry feelings with father into exercise.

In 1990 Elena ran the London marathon. She had never thought of running outside of a gym, but experienced the pleasure of running with thousands of others instead of running only with herself as a liberation. This began an exploration of how she might use her fitness as a means of communicating with the outside world rather than cutting it off. In the short term her husband, William, was alarmed by these changes. His beautiful wife seemed to have been replaced by a woman far more active than he had expected. As she changed and reinvested her energies, so he too had to change to keep up with her.

~

Object love

Even inanimate objects can become the receptacles of our love. Indeed some people find it much safer to invest their love in art, or an object of beauty, rather than risk the more turbulent waters of loving people. This love requires acquisition, we yearn to own the loved object or at least have it readily available to us. Collectors represent a dedicated group of object lovers. For each of them a particular kind of object takes centre stage, and is imbued with great meaning and positive feelings. They like to be amongst their loved objects, and can spend hours happily rearranging them in a form of relationship with them. Many people who are quite capable of normal loving relationships with others nonetheless like to take the peace and solitude of object love for some time in their lives. As children, we have transitional objects such as blankets or teddy bears which make us feel safe and secure. As adults we move those emotions onto rather more grown-up objects, paintings, a stamp collection, trains. This form of object love seems to appeal more to men than women. Many men actually use it as a hiding place from the demands of love relationships.

~

Billy has been collecting postcards since his mid-teens. Now in his forties, he has a magnificent collection, of which he is rightly proud. However, his wife Suzy finds herself hating this collection and often feeling that she and the children are in competition with it for Billy's attention. So much of his time is spent in arranging and cataloguing, chasing new 'finds' and corresponding with other enthusiasts, that he does sometimes neglect his family. When pushed he will admit that he finds relationships difficult and that in particular he found his children 'upsetting and inexplicable'. He says that he loves them deeply but cannot find ways to express this. Much of the energy which Billy might have used for overcoming his relationship difficulties and expressing his emotions to his family is instead directed into his collecting behaviour. When he talks about his collection he has no difficulty at all in making you aware of just how deep his emotional commitment to it is. It represents a safe non-challenging object for his feelings, something he can control, own and possess, so unlike the struggles of relating to other people.

~

Times of pure happiness often take us by surprise, a

sight of an object of great beauty, something which 'speaks' to our inner needs. The pulse of love experienced at those moments, though fleeting, may leave the marks of an indelible memory, a happy moment to be treasured. These experiences may represent moments of completely untarnished love invested momentarily, so that there is no danger of it being less than ideal. Such moments encapsulate a perfect match between our inner and outer worlds, an inner experience beautifully represented by an external object.

~

Not long after leaving a long-term destructive relationship, Sara was suddenly aware of a ray of spring sunshine penetrating her room and lighting up previously dark corners. This simple moment felt like magic. She described it as suddenly seeing that she loved to be free and the sunlight seemed, at that moment, to be a perfect symbol for new life, hope and warmth. She said 'I woke up to the fact that I still had love, alive, inside of me.'

~

Sunlight has, of course, been a symbol of hope for many centuries and across cultures. It has a life-enhancing property, and although people describe themselves as 'loving' sunshine in a flippant way, it is probably true that most of us have deep feelings of gratitude when we feel its warmth. However, such love is not constant; too much sunshine and heat and we will quickly change our feelings into hope for rain!

Love of causes

We invest meaning and emotions into many aspects of our environment. Loving and caring for it on the one hand, using and abusing it on the other. We talk of love of country and even sometimes refer to our own country as 'motherland'. The depth of this love is reflected in people's willingness to die in order to preserve a part of the earth for themselves. However, such love always has another and more dependent aspect which does reach back to the roots of our earliest relationship with mother. Most wars are fought with a zealous form of love and belief invested in a place or a religion, or both. Alongside of such fighting, such dependent commitment to a cause, there lurks the other side of the love coin, the fury and the destructiveness. War may represent the most extreme variety of the love/hate dichotomy. It allows us to turn all the loving feelings inwards to our own group, and all the negative hostile feelings out onto another group. So irrational is this process that it makes it possible for normal people, like you or me, to live peacefully with neighbours for forty years and then, overnight, become their murderers, their rapists, their torturers. That we might have the potential to behave in these ways, which represent the most awful possibilities in life, is usually hidden by the thin veneer of civilization. However, in every love relationship there lurks the other hideous extreme.

Investing our love in concepts, ideas, politics or religion allows us to experience fundamentally 'earthy' emotions in a more spiritual, intellectual or idealistic way. Spiritual and intellectual aspects of life are of importance for many, and therefore great satisfaction comes from investing love energy in these causes.

Love can take different forms and have different meanings, depending on our emotional age. Early love is about attachment, bonding and a fear of separation. Later, issues of power, autonomy and control feature heavily in our love relationships. Finally sexuality develops, investing love with passion. We can invest each or all of these developmental phases of love into concepts and ideas, religions, philosophies and politics.

Thus we may speak of ourselves as attached to an idea, and experience acute anxiety if people try to argue against our investment in the idea. In some ways that idea has become an abstract form of a transitional object, something to hang onto in a world which would otherwise be experienced as too threatening to bear. It may seem strange to regard a political affiliation as the adult abstract form of a teddy bear, but in many ways it serves a similar emotional purpose. It helps to make an otherwise meaningless and unpredictable life into an attached, committed and secure existence.

Investment of love energy at the middle developmental phase always means that the love is flavoured by issues of power and control. This is clearly the case in concepts of politics and religion, for instance. This form of love may bind someone to an idea by insisting on inner control, a power over the self which restricts gratification. Such feats of love are performed in religious fasting, for instance, or in restricting sexuality to certain times, places and relationships. By contrast, these ideas can be riddled with the notion of achieving power and control over others. If you love a concept you have little emotional need to question its validity, and thus your commitment can blind you to the true needs or beliefs of others. Many political and religious ideas have ridden rough shod over millions of people, demonstrating the evil opposite to love. It is frightening to see how illogical and closed off from reasoned argument we can become when love-invested in an idea. Such ideas are usually 'sold' as a form of salvation for mankind, thus giving them a superficial credibility which rapidly becomes unassailable.

Sexuality is often invested in politics and religion. In many ways, from the outside, it would seem as if politics captures, enhances and magnifies sexuality, while religion builds itself a philosophical barricade against it. However, psychoanalytically both could be seen as a form of defence against truly person-related sexuality, making it a more object-focused form of sexual love instead.

Those who invest a great deal of love energy into concepts tend to have less available energy for relationships with people. In many ways the hierarchies of both the political and religious worlds build themselves a form of life which then acts as an alibi for this detachment from human relationships. The relationships they develop will be required to 'feed' them and their convictions, first and foremost. Clearly this can be hard on partners and children, particularly if they are not so invested in the same concept.

Henri had been a politician in local government for fifteen years. His wife, Josie and their children, Sam, aged eight and Hugo, aged twelve, saw little of Henri. When he was at home he insisted on being their focus. His work, his beliefs had to be important to them all. When he was away he gave little thought to them or their problems and pleasures. When Josie said that she wanted a divorce his first comment was, 'But what effect will that have on my work?' In his campaigning he gave voice to strong committed feelings about the importance of 'the family', and yet he had very limited capacities himself to relate to his own. He did not experience those limits as in any way questioning his intellectual beliefs.

~

The deeper the loving commitment to the concept, the less the capacity to relate to other people becomes. We can all recognize that individual who is capable of compassion to other people even when immersed in conceptual commitment. These individuals are rare, however, and there are many more examples of those who are embedded in a committed political or religious system being inhumane, apparently without conscience, because they believe they are acting, for instance, from their love of God. Such people tend to give their particular philosophy, politics or religion a poor image to the rest of us, often separating us from any form of attachment to their beliefs by their very commitment.

The notion that it is healthiest to hold on only loosely

to those things, beliefs and people that you love is demonstrated over and over again. Overattachment, too great a pursuit of power and control, too much focus either for or against sexuality, and the love invested can so easily go sour.

9

Losing Love

Ebbs and flows of love

Many forms of love are not in fact stable states, but are in flux. Sometimes love matures, changing form and intensity in order to preserve itself. Sometimes it fades and loses its lustre, or sometimes it just dies. Sometimes the person we love changes in a way to which we cannot adjust, and sometimes we lose the person we love through death or disease. A belief can suddenly be shattered in the loss of love, the certainty to which we previously subscribed is suddenly removed.

The comings and goings of love form a central thread in our lives. The changing love for our parents over many years becomes interwoven with the love of sexual partners and friends in our adult life, and with the love of our own children if we have them. The pattern which we weave is unique for each of us, and only partially under our control. Most of us would not choose to lose love at all throughout life; the loss is a painful and anxiety-provoking experience. It causes us to take stock of all of life, because love is such a crucial element in our understanding of ourselves, our self-esteem and our happiness.

Love is not an easily controlled emotion. We cannot

will it to stop or start simply because we want it to. It is such a changeable experience that the very attempt to hold and control it may break the spell. Lovers often wish that they could hold a moment of their love for ever, so perfect is that moment for them both. But even as they give voice to such a wish the moment moves on. Love has to survive many disillusionments and disappointments in its journey to maturity. Life is full of events, chances and surprises which have the capacity to intensify or destroy the love of those involved.

In therapy it is not unusual to hear people who have been hurt or humiliated by those they love questioning how much disillusionment or disappointment is normal in the lifetime of any love. 'Am I being too trusting, too forgiving?' they ask. Or 'Should I battle on despite the emotional pain in an attempt to retrive love again?' For each of us these questions are constantly evaluated during a lifetime.

~

Dina had been sexually abused by the father she loved throughout much of her childhood. She continued to love him until she saw a programme on television describing the damage that childhood sexual abuse could produce in the survivor. At that moment she descibed a sudden knowledge: 'I had to decide whether I loved him or myself. I knew with blinding clarity that I could not love us both. For the first time in my life I decided to love me, which meant that I stopped loving him.'

~

Annette witnessed the murder of her partner by her son, Tim, then eighteen years old. She said, 'Even in the moment of horror, as we both realized what he had done, I knew I would stand by him. But equally I knew that this was duty and obligation. He was my child, however bad. I didn't know then, I still don't know now, whether I will ever love and trust him again.'

~

Natalie had forgiven Charlie's infidelities for twenty-four years of marriage. 'He always said that the other women weren't important,' she explained, 'and so I continued to love him. One day I thought: they may not be important to you but they are to me. Just having the thought seemed enough to throw a switch in my head. One moment I loved him and the next I didn't.'

~

Mary and Bill lost their third child as a cot death when she was just three months old. They grieved in very different and therefore separate ways. Bill was mostly quiet but every few weeks would explode in fury about a trivial incident in the home. Mary felt empty and desolate and longed for Bill to hold and comfort her. He seemed unable to do this. Their loss eroded the previously close and loving relationship. Gradually they lost any sense of connection or purpose in their relationship. 'I couldn't remember what loving Bill felt like,' Mary said, 'as if the distance between us extinguished any memory of what had gone before.'

~

Religion had always been important for James, helping him come to terms with the loss of his parents in his late thirties. It took him out to India as a missionary. The poverty and disease that surrounded him there began to shake his faith in a loving God. Increasingly the words of the Bible or prayers seemed meaningless in the face of his day-to-day experience. 'I had loved a loving God,' he explained. 'As I began to perceive him as less loving I too became less loving of him.'

~

We cannot control the ebbing and flowing of our loving feelings. In the above examples there was, for each person, an event or a series of events which formed a turning-point in the person's feelings. However, sometimes love dies or fades and we have no explanation or reason for this change. Perhaps we register many little details of the loved one, trivial in themselves, which add up eventually to something important enough to extinguish love. Perhaps we hide, from ourselves and others, questions and anxieties about loved ones, but these uncertainties eat up love from within so that one day we wake up and find it gone. The fading of love may have nothing to do with the loved one or their behaviour, but rather stem from our own past experiences. Love lives can sometimes run as if to script for a person, but that script is an unconscious momentum, turning-off the loving feelings without leaving an explanation.

~

Claudia was on the point of a second divorce when she realized that she was repeating a pattern. Friends told her that it was true that she had married two difficult men and that it was easy to imagine why she might wish to be divorced from them. What alerted her however was that she was rerunning a life story at exactly ten-year intervals. She wondered how it was possible to love such exacting partners for exactly the same number of years each and then suddenly find yourself out of love and eager for divorce. Looking back ten years prior to her first divorce she realized that she also made a big and sudden life-change at that point. Looking back a further ten years, to the time when she was twelve, she was amazed to realize that not just the year but the month of each of these events matched the month her elder brother had died of a chronic illness.

Friends suggested to her that by loving and marrying difficult and disturbed men she was reliving her relationship with the sick brother, who was also demanding of attention, leaving very little care or family love for Claudia. However, the brother's death had released Claudia from that relationship and meant that she received much more attention and support. Thus she expected, unconsciously, to be able to 'kill off' the sick marriages too, according to her own internalized time schedule. In discussion with her first husband he commented that he had felt 'murdered' by Claudia at the time of their divorce. 'You put up with so much, nothing was more difficult than before but suddenly you just shut up and were gone. I never really understood why it had to be so quick and clean and absolute.'

Eventually Claudia did divorce the second husband, and went into therapy to help increase her understanding of why she chose sick partners, so that she could prevent the pattern repeating itself again.

~

If we are unable to afford much control or comprehension over our own loving feelings, those of others for us are even more difficult to manipulate or understand. Many people exert much of their emotional energy throughout life trying to make people love them. This is a most insecure emotional bedrock for any life. However good, loving, kind and patient a partner is, they cannot ensure that the other will continue to love them. We chose our loved ones for many hidden reasons, as well as those we could give voice to. The partner can never know what is on the other's 'hidden agenda' for love. As a consequence, trying hard or manipulating is always a shot in the dark to preserve love.

~

Katriona believed that the way you kept your husband loving you was to be sexually cold and withholding for much of the time. This was what her mother had taught her, and it seemed to work in her parents' marriage. She could not know that her father had had many affairs to which her mother turned a blind eye, because it was a well-kept family secret. Katriona's husband found a similar solution to his frustrations at home. Having been brought up in a very similar household to Katriona's, this did not seem an unusual state of a marriage. However, in the course of his work he met a woman who excited him more both sexually and intellectually than he had ever imagined possible, and he fell in love. He realized during the falling in love 'process' that this was an entirely new experience for him. Unlike both his own and Katriona's parents, the way they had chosen to secure their marriage had in fact opened the door to the elements of its destruction.

~

When faced with the freshness and intensity of new love, an older love rooted in obligation or duty can easily wither. We may feel guilty about the pain we cause when this happens, or perhaps angry about the disruption that this change causes in our lives, but for the most part we are helpless, like leaves in the wind, tossed by the heady feelings, the promises that new love holds seductively out to us. It is easy to moralize about such occasions, indeed many of our social, cultural and religious laws try to surround us with behavioural bounda-

ries to protect us from the sweeping changes that adult
love can induce. And all these sanctions are in spite of
the fact that more adult relationships than ever before
are demonstrating that love is not for ever, but only
troublingly precarious.

Learning from the loss of love

Are we more open and honest these days about the loss
of love in adult relationships? Has the quality of love
between adult partners changed? Do we now expect
more from love? Are we more touched by disappointment or disillusionment than previous generations?
It is more important now than ever before to understand
the phenomena surrounding the loss of love in committed relationships. Despite the fact that second or
third loves hold out magical possibilities for each individual, we know statistically that these loving relationships are even more vulnerable to change and collapse
than the first. Described as the triumph of optimism
over experience, the new love seems to sweep away the
capacity to make rational judgements about its quality.
Far from learning from loving relationships and their
failures, it often seems as if people are more eager to
embrace a new love when an old one is perceived as
having failed them. But does love fail us or do we fail it?
How often do we allow ourselves to fall in love in what
we hope will be a recuperation from previous disappointments? How often do we allow ourselves to believe
that this time we have found the magic 'it', that this
relationship is different?

In a recent conversation with an experienced coun-

sellor for the marriage guidance organization Relate I
asked what quality made the difference between the
relationships that could be salvaged and those that
seemed doomed. 'In the short term,' she answered,
'one partner has to be big enough to forgive. In
the long term they both have to find forgiveness.
Forgiveness and tolerance that work both ways."

In many ways it would seem then as if the capacity to
be relatively unconditional in love is not only esential
between parents and children, but also crucial in adult to
adult relationships. The problem with this is that we
each have belief systems which are important to our
sense of self. If a loved one breaks that belief system,
then we have to be remarkably flexible, perhaps too
flexible for our own good, to be able to forgive.
Breaches of faith in relationships cause terrible pain, the
more invested in love the greater the pain of any form
of betrayal. However much we might theorize about the
importance of forgiveness in preserving love, some
betrayals are beyond a normal human capacity for forgiving. There is also a wide gulf between forgiving and
forgetting. Forgiving usually means being able to continue to love in a relationship which has, for ever,
changed its quality, precisely because something cannot
be forgotten.

Psychologically, forgiving seems to be one of the most
elusive states, impossible to impose on ourselves or
others and often taking a long time while pain subsides
and a different reality about love seeps in. When we
think of love we rarely think of forgiveness in the same
breath: we make assumptions that if we love and are

loved then there will be little or nothing to forgive. In the famous words from *Love Story*, 'Love means never having to say you are sorry.' And yet for most loving partners there are occasions when it is important to apologize, to accept and acknowledge we have got something wrong, said something unreasonably hurtful, or done something outrageous. Unless partners can see and talk about such events, bitterness and resentment soon come to fill the emotional spaces once filled with love. In the face of long-term bitterness, forgiveness and healing seem impossible.

Can we care for our love relationships in adulthood in ways that take some responsibility for the maintenance of the love? When people talk of 'working at it' what do they mean? I remember a telegram read out at a wedding years ago that said, 'We wish you whatever you want and need, but don't be greedy.' In the early days of love it is difficult to imagine that that love will wear thin, become strained and impoverished, feel like a burden rather than an inspiration. But for each of us there are times when the love we hoped would hold and take care of us does the reverse, draining and hurting us instead.

We need to be aware of the development of our need for love and our capacity to give love. So fundamental to the building of a personality are these basic love experiences, that those who have sadly missed early opportunities to develop love will always seem rather hollow, needy but never satiated. Such people may make rapid and intense emotional bonds throughout adult life, desperately trying to capture a love they have never known, but they are unlikely to ever be satisfied and therefore become quickly disillusioned in the face of even trivial disappointments.

In the western world we are making greater and greater demands on adult loving relationships. They are expected to be emotionally, sexually and intellectually sustaining, whatever the external realities of the couples' lives – the stresses and strains and the ongoing developmental changes such as having children. I have often been struck by just how similar many people's disappointments in relationships are. We each think our disappointment a uniquely personal affair, and yet time and again the universality of the complaints suggests that this is not the case.

~

Tabitha described feeling low and run-down for most of her six-year relationship with Nicki. She felt as if she was being drained by Nicki's emotional needs and however hard she tried to get her own needs met something always got in the way. From the moment she decided to move out she began to feel better and stronger. Meanwhile Nicki became depressed in Tabitha's absence.

~

See-sawing of a couple's emotions is a common state, where by an unconsious agreement one member of the couple 'carries' the depression for them both at any one time. The 'carer' then feels depressed and drained when they are together. This person often tolerates the situation for years, because taking care of someone else does fulfil some of their own emotional requirements. It allows them to feel the stronger of the two, useful, kind and adult. Meanwhile the 'cared for' gets much emotional support and has considerable manipulative power within the relationship, but has to pay the price of being sick or childlike in some way to keep the arrangement going. Sooner or later something happens to change this dynamic balance. Often either the carer simply becomes tired and drained, or the 'cared for' grows up and becomes better. Such couples separate but often find it difficult to stay separated. The 'cared for' becomes tired and depressed by the responsibilities of being grown-up or well, and the 'carer' feels like less of a good person when not caring for someone. Thus the original attraction is rekindled. In many couples this interaction is a complex sequence of events because there are 'carer' and 'cared for' aspects to them both.

Maintaining love does require that at least some emotional needs are met. Those who have low expectations that needs will be met – based either on childhood experience or their own independent personality – will continue to have low expectations of needs being met in adult relationships. This will make them undemanding in relationships, and therefore they often chose to love partners who are not very forthcoming with love themselves. Although such relationships may not seem fulfilling to at least one partner from the outside, they are often remarkably stable, unless the partner who considers themselves to be 'not needy' changes. This may be an internalized change. For instance at consciousness-raising workshops women often discover that they are denying their needs and therefore these needs are not met. Once they stop denying their needs their partner's limited capacity to give, love becomes exposed. External changes too can precipitate someone previously not demanding to need greater attention, a loss or trauma for instance, and again if the partner is incapable of responding to the change then the underlying flaw in the relationship becomes exposed.

At the opposite end of the spectrum, those who have been brought up to be intensely demanding in relationships – and often highly critical as well – find partners who wish to be emotionally generous. Such generosity may wear thin over the years, however. In these unbalanced giving and taking situations the difference between perception of needs may only be marginal at the beginning of the relationship. However it is at the start of relationships that we train the other to know what they can expect from us and what they can expect to get away with. In this way small differences can become enlarged, as one partner gets into the habit of demanding and the other of responding. This may explain why relationships that have argumentative early phases during the first year or two are likely to find more well-balanced stability eventually. Couples who fail to 'stick up for themselves' in the early days of relationships are more likely to allow their relationships to become dangerously unbalanced. For many, however, the idea of 'sticking up for yourself' in a loving relationship feels alien, as if it betrays the more idealistic notions of what the other person's love might contain for you. Many need to believe that if they are good and loving enough then that guarantees the goodness and love in the partner too.

Love and battle of the sexes

At present the majority of people pushing for divorce are women. In therapy I see many women who are unhappy with the quality of their emotional lives with the men they love. There is no doubt that women's equality has made giant strides forward in the outer world of education and work (even though many women still work for low wages and little or no social status). In the home, however, little has changed in terms of housework, childcare and emotional support. Feminists have pointed out that the central adult 'love relationship' of our society, marriage, is also the major remaining instrument of oppression of men towards women. It is at home that women work for no wages, are given little or no reward for their input, and are often remarkably invisible. The children for whom they take a lioness' share of the responsibility usually still bear the father's surname, for instance.

The need to love men which so many women experience makes sexual oppression different to all others. It is the only state of oppression in which the oppressed person is compelled as much by inner desires as by outer forces to share their emotional and physical worlds with an oppressor. For most couples, such relationships are made possible by a psychological disconnection in their minds from what happens outside, in the patriarchal state, and what happens inside, in the love relationship. However, this disconnection cannot be maintained if there is any hint within the relationship of the power differential between men and women. As soon as that power differential becomes apparent, to one or both parties, love becomes an alibi for a much more business like state of affairs. Many supposed love relationships do function as an unconsciously agreed deal. Usually this involves the man 'taking care' of the external world of income and boundaries around the family, while the woman 'takes care' of the internal world of emotions and needs of family members.

Such 'deals' are almost always described as love relationships, at least in their early days, because to describe them more completely would be to reveal the gulf between the partners' contributions to and rewards from such unions. Most men still earn more money than women, have more status in society, whatever they choose to do, and have more external power in terms of politics, law and culture. Thus, however liberated a woman may feel as an individual, the taking of a male partner will usually place her in a relationship in which she has less external power.

Meanwhile, heterosexual relationships do seem to have a powerful capacity to regress men more than women. Perhaps we should not be surprised given that, for both men and women, our earliest memories are of physical closeness with a woman, our mother. This memory is unconsciously stirred in men by physical closeness with a woman. Such feelings can evoke both bliss and intense anxiety, because the infant experiences both the gratification of its wishes and their frustration in his emotional experience with mother. Many men sexualize all their needs, so as to deny the powerful emotional reverberations that relating to women arouses. Others acknowledge emotional needs and wish to 'own' the woman involved in a social state, which can then ease fears about her frustrating them. Although we are no longer culturally comfortable with the concept of one partner in a love relationship 'owning' the other, the emotional responses of both partners in marriages often seems still to give credence to such a concept, whether they would consciously acknowledge it or not.

In its most extreme form, the man will attempt to control all aspects of the 'woman he loves'. His needs will determine where they live, who they socialize with, how the daily routine is planned. If even the smallest detail of the plan is changed, he will fly into infantile rage. The likelihood of such rage becomes greater in the presence of alcohol or drugs. As a society we want to believe that this no longer happens in the context of a love relationship, and yet every day we are presented with external evidence that women are treated to more violence, abuse, danger and death within their adult love relationship than anywhere else. The mystery of why women put up with such treatment is often obscured by them saying 'But I love him,' or 'But he loves me.'

Even in the least extreme forms, many women regard the men they love as more childish than themselves. 'Boys never grow up' is an enshrined assumption in our culture. Alongside of that is a deeply-held belief that men, for all their external power and dominance, need protecting from the inner world of emotions and demands.

Today's educated woman has a different set of assumptions, which run parallel to these basic social assumptions. Thus, she enters a love relationship with a man hoping that such distortions are a thing of the past, and new male/female relationships are in line with her new assumptions of rights and equalities. Many men also have the same conscious hopes that their ability to relate lovingly will, for instance, be very different to their father's or grandfather's. However, the human psyche is a complex thing, full of unexpected and unconsious intentions. Whether we wish it or not, we are psychologically touched by the patterns of relating between men and women of past generations. Each couple, however determined, is psychologically sucked back into previous cultural assumptions much more forcibly than they would ever predict. Thus, the relationships we all invest such hope in as different become strangely the same. It is often these relationships which women now want to divorce themselves from.

As we are allowed, even encouraged, to believe that our love relationships are personal rather than sociological happenings, we often diagnose the failure of a relationship in terms of an individual partner's failings. Taking a broader view, there are social trends which suggest that women's assumptions about the nature of love have moved faster and more completely than men's. This is hardly surprising, as these changes benefit women and, in the eyes of many, have little benefit – indeed possibly disadvantage – men. Sociologically, women may be falling out of love with a particular picture of masculinity. This does not prevent them falling in love with an individual man, who they believe to be different, but then they may not want to love him if and when he is seen to be 'the same'.

The loss of love in gay relationships

I have seen a particular kind of enforced quiet suffering in homosexual couples who fall out of love. Because they are still treated as second-class relationships, with little or no social validity, so their loss is given less credence. While they might meet support and comfort from other gay friends, they are less likely than their heterosexual colleagues to be given recognition as someone who has lost the love of an important other. Their distress is as great, but often not externally marked in any way.

~

Jane is a schoolteacher who has always hidden her lesbianism from colleagues for fear of what exposure might do to her career prospects. She had an intensely loving relationship with Jackie for eight years, perhaps all the more intense and committed because of the secrecy with which much of the relationship was conducted. During a holiday, Jackie met and fell in love with a woman in France, and did not return home with Jane. Despite feeling devastated, shocked and numb, Jane felt that she had no alternative but to return to school a week later and pretend that nothing terrible had happened. In this way she began what she later described as the worst year in her life, when she pretended normality for school hours and then descended into deep troughs of grief and despair in the evenings and weekends. As this process began to abate she felt angry at the extent to which she had had to split off 'acceptable' and 'unacceptable' parts of herself. Feeling unacceptable about her sexuality in a large part of her life meant that her grief was as unacceptable as her previous happiness had been. A naive counsellor attempted to suggest to her that this was her problem and that if she could find the courage to be honest about her sexuality such a split would not have happened. Jane, however, had the evidence of what had happened to another lesbian colleague who had been more open; she had met severe opposition to her career.

~

Loss through death

The greatest loss of love comes when a loved person dies. Many accounts of this trauma have been written, detailing the phases of numbness, pain, anger and eventual integration of the loss. The passage of these phases differs for each person and for each relationship. A sudden death may cause more initial numbness as the mind tries to protect itself from the overwhelming nature of the loss. A long protracted illness may leave a confused grief, with relief that a loved one's suffering is over intermingled with the sense of loss. For most of us it is easier to let go of a parent in death than it is to let go of a child; easier to grieve a relationship in which our feelings have been clear-cut than one in which we have felt ambiguous.

For most people, grief is not a chain-reaction in which we go smoothly from one state of mind to the next, but rather a switchback ride of feelings, often swinging rapidly from one state to another. A widow recently described her grieving as a 'tidal' process, as feelings came and went. As a society we have lost most of the rituals connected with grieving, and have the unreal expectations that people can cope with the loss of a partner, parent, or child within a few weeks. We expect them to return to work and once again 'fit in' with social needs. Because we all fear the devastation of loss, we are unwilling to be exposed to the effects of loss on others. For many, the pressures of social expectations mean that grief goes 'underground' in our mind, to re-emerge as a sudden wave of anxiety about our own physical health, or as depression. Grief can be delayed in its expression for many years, until a further loss triggers the feelings off again.

Crucially, many people do not expect grief to be an angry emotion, and therefore have difficulty acknowledging their anger to others.

~

Dolly was widowed after fifty-two years of marriage. As she began silently to rage to herself about the treatment Ted had received, she thought that she might be going mad. Then her anger began to generalize until her family and friends were the objects of her internalized assaults. In order to protect others from this increasing fury she cut herself off from any contact with them. In her loneliness the rage got worse. Eventually, taken out for the day by her daughter, Dolly erupted in a vicious stream of criticism and complaint. Although shocked, her daughter, Pamela, recognized in her mother a more extreme form of what she herself had been feeling since her father's death.

~

Anger is often displaced onto healthcare workers − the professionals who 'fail' − onto God, onto the family or onto self. With every death there is always a sense of 'if only . . .', as if we could rerun it and avoid the loss. Anger makes us want to believe that it is someone's fault rather than fate, which feels too big and terrifying to allow. Sometimes this leads people into generously altruistic behaviour: 'I don't want anyone else to ever feel as badly as I do.'

Research suggests that the physical health of the surviving partner is more at risk in the year immediately after bereavement. The sense of apathy, low self-esteem, of being no value any more, of feeling guilt-ridden, make the person vulnerable emotionally and physically. While bereavement is a normal part of life, that does not mean that we do not require support, love and comfort to help us through the most intense feelings. People need permission to grieve, confirmation that their feelings are normal, not madness, and that these feelings have a purpose, which is eventually to allow the loss to take an appropriate position in the context of our total life experience.

Sometimes we invest our love energy in experiences, places or belief systems, rather than (or alongside) personal relationships. If and when such things lose their symbolic value for us, that loss is often experienced as deeply as the loss of a person.

～

Anthony had been a determined mountaineer since adolescence. He would happily admit that he loved mountains and felt at his best when climbing them. He did not question the symbolism of such an attachment any more than we might question why we fall in love with a particular person. Then, in his mid-thirties, he was in a climbing party in which three younger climbers were killed. He described being overwhelmed by a sense of betrayal that the mountains he had loved had turned out to be such malevolent places. Although friends pointed out that it was not the mountains that had changed, Anthony could not shake-off the sense of betrayal, which filled him with hate for the countryside he had once loved. In therapy he explored the symbolism of his love of mountains, of how much his sense of mastery of life generally was based on his ability to conquer such harsh and unforgiving places.

～

Just like Anthony, we all come to love that which we need to love in order to make us feel bearably comfortable in life. We choose our love objects with a psychological purpose, although we may be unconscious of it. If the love object fails to meet that need, so we will withdraw our love and feel diminished rather than enhanced by the object. Such capacity to love symbolically gives much colour and meaning to our lives. It may give us purpose, motivation and confidence in a world which would otherwise feel threateningly chaotic. Like all love, however, it is uncertain and unpredictable; at the moment of embracing it we have also to embrace the inner knowledge that we may well lose it eventually.

Conclusion

This exploration of love has highlighted the many contradictions inherent in this simple word. Far from being a single emotion, love is a complex emotional state in which almost any other human emotion can also reside. Despite knowing this intellectually, when presented with the word most of us still immediately think of romance and happiness rather than acknowledging the more difficult aspects of the same experience. This leaves us open to disillusionment, disappointment, even despair, when reality strikes – as it always eventually will – into our love fantasies.

As love is a central thread in all of our relationships, both to people and ideas and objects, the fact that we find it hard to accept it in its entirety makes us all vulnerable to experiencing it in a depressing way, as someone or something which lets us down. If we wish to preserve our hopes for the fantasized perfect love, we have to believe that it is the person or the idea that has failed us rather than our one-sided vision of what love is capable of being. So we start again with a new relationship, a new idea or commitment, still carrying our idealistic views on love and thus just as vulnerable the next time around.

Reality would have us acknowledge that the love between parents and children can never be perfect, for instance. That there will always be failures to live up to the high hopes of idealized parenting. But how hard it is to accept that wonderful parenting cannot put right all the problems a child ever inherited, or that a wonderful child cannot magically make their parents' world a perfect place. We want the lover we adore today to be exactly the same idealized person tomorrow, and every day. The husband and wife both want to maintain the optimistic hopes of the wedding. Behind closed doors we all experience the disillusionment separately and to different extents. The love we hoped for and thought we might have found has turned out to be a mixed affair, with good and bad bits, happiness and unhappiness, grief and joy, all parcelled together.

If, as children, we have grown to understand and accept that love is a flawed and human state rather than a secure and perfect place, then we can cope with the disappointments of adult love more easily. However, many people still feel that children should never be exposed to marital realities, for instance, but should be encouraged always to believe that their parents' marriage is a form of relational perfection which they have, in adult life, to attain. As a society, we put great pressures on parents to get it right with their children, with little acknowledgement that this is impossible and that good parenting is more to do with learning to fail gracefully than living up to ideals! Perhaps we cry at weddings because we all know, however subconsciously, that we are witnessing the high hopes of the ideal which cannot and will not be sustained for very long in a real relationship.

What we have to see clearly is that love as an experience will never conform to our fantasies, hopes or even our needs. When we try to squeeze it into what we want or expect we rapidly squeeze the life out of it. We can pretend, sometimes for years, that we have it under control, but sooner or later someone or something will give lie to this. Love has a life of its own. It comes when least bidden, refuses to go when convenient, and will resist our greatest efforts to make it appear when we need it. Although it is the golden thread which holds our lives together in some meaningful whole, it weaves in its own way, in its own time and its own place.

Life without the magical experience of the first rush of love, unblemished by any experience or reality confrontation, would be a sad place. Not only our own loves but those of friends and relatives lift our lives momentarily into hopefulness. We often respond to the marriages of public figures by reverberating to their own happiness. Their subsequent disillusionments touch us too. It is a complex task, however, to be able to enjoy the moment and yet also keep in mind some sort of real image of love's future.

For some, the disappointment in love is so early in life, so intense and so painful that they never take the risk of loving again. Their relationships may be sensible, stable, the sort of solid marriage, for instance, that survives on a pragmatic basis, but lacks the zest of the loving experience. In many cultures these sorts of marriages are encouraged, as they make better building-blocks for a secure extended family. Of course it may be possible for a mature form of love to grow in these relationships, based on each partner fulfilling their roles in an honourable way, of coming to like and respect each other. Perhaps, in western cultures, we have been over-exposed to the idealized forms of love. It is so yearned for that it sells anything from fizzy drinks to political parties. Most love stories stop at the perfect moment of love, few have the courage to go on to the 'ever after' bits, because they know we might turn off when we discover it is not too happy.

I know many adults who would question whether love exists. Is it merely a figment of our imagination? Do we construct it within ourselves, based on material we are fed as children? We see our parents' relationship, and presume that it is wonderful and thus want some of that wonder. We see fairy-tales which end happily. As we grow through adolescence the hunt for the perfect partner intensifies. By now we have an inner assumption about love, who we can love, what it will feel like, what will happen next. We have written the script and search out the other actors. But then we discover that those selected actors have also written their own, different, scripts. Whose is the 'true' love script?

Certainly it is clear that even children from unhappy parental partnerships still maintain assumptions about the possibility of marital bliss. Indeed, many children from unhappy homes will search even more hopefully, and sometimes desperately, for the love partner with whom to build the perfect family. Clearly they are able to construct within their inner world a very different and more hopeful version of adult love than they have ever been exposed to. Sadly, however, while maintaining high hopes and goals consciously, their unconscious mind betrays them when it comes to the selection of partners. Freud called this 'repetition compulsion'. If something goes wrong in our early lives we feel compelled to rerun it again later with other people in the hope of getting it right next time.

~

Sally's father repeatedly told her that he did not want or like her. As she grew, Sally watched her mother's life get ever harder, and never saw any parental love expressed between mother and father. Nevertheless, she left school to marry at seventeen, convinced that she had met the man to release her from such unhappiness. Within weeks of marriage, Sally realized she had swapped from being her mother's helpless witness to being in exactly the same position as her mother. This filled her with horror, and paralysed any capacity to think about herself or constructing her own life. She lived in this state for a number of years, compulsively repeating her mother's existence and desperate to find a way to make it better.

Then Sally met Joe during a training day at work. She fell in love immediately and felt like a romantic heroine. This state of intense happiness lasted a mere three months, until she discovered that Joe was gay. In the moment of her discovery, not only did she see that she had constructed a hero to rescue her based only very loosely on what Joe had to offer, but also, with the sort of crushing insight disappointment can sometimes provoke, that her father too had been homosexual. Later she described a form of relief mixed with great sadness. She had repeated her childhood relationships to the point when she could make some sort of sense of them, and this released her from her compulsion to put them right.

~

For women it is often the mother/daughter relationship which is the most difficult one to understand and feel secure within. This does not stop many mothers and daughters trying time after time to find the hoped-for union between them. Women have to learn to relate in what is still a patriarchal context, both with the family and the wider society. As this context tends to undermine the importance of women in all fields, it is particularly undermining to the formation of fulfilling relationships between women. Whatever the achievements of feminism the work of the home is still falling on the shoulders of the mother. Many women still make this their lifetime occupation, others fit it in between jobs, careers, hobbies and other ambitions. Either way, it remains unpaid and, for the most part, unrewarded by any form of feedback. This vision of mother and her life is not easy or attractive to most daughters. Shere Hite conducted a survey in the United States in 1989 which suggested that 72 per cent of daughters were desperate not to grow up to be like their mothers or live similar lives.

This does not make an easy starting-place for any relationship. Given that it is a relationship that is bound to be coloured by competition and by early battles for control and autonomy, it is a minefield for hostility and mistrust rather than love. Over the last three decades, the variety of life-choices for women has expanded considerably. This has made the tension between mothers and daughters even greater. Mothers would need to be saints not to envy their daughters, newly-won freedoms, and it is all too easy for the daughters to forget, or to never know, that it was their mothers and their grandmothers who won them those freedoms. Perhaps if we could thank our mothers more for these freedom gifts, they might envy us less.

Acknowledging mothers as normal people, who make mistakes, have failed to give us the parenting we wanted, express opinions we could do without, but who have made valuable, all too often dismissed contributions to our own lives is often the hardest step in growing-up female. To let daughters flourish into whatever they wish within their own time, even if they seem to have to make all the old mistakes over again for themselves, is often the hardest bit about being a mother to a daughter. Only in this arena, however, can the love relationship which is so central to most women's lives take its rightful place. It is only when this relationship has slotted into place that women can hope to make realistic loving relationships not only with other women, but also with men.

Life is full of the rich variety of love relationships we can have, with children, adults, parents, lovers, partners, and friends. Each has its own flavour, its own range of possibilities, and its own limitations. Along with human relationships we also have the capacity to love ideas, symbols and commitments. To have a life which can repay our efforts we need to invest in a wide diversity of loving experiences and not place all our hopes into one love 'basket'. Wide investment protects us from the vagaries of love, the ups and downs inherent in its nature, the disappointments and disillusionments.

Love cannot save us from life's given parameters. We are born at a time, place and to people we cannot dictate. We come ready-programmed with a genetic code which gives a template to our size, shape, personality, intelligence and physio-psychological vulnerabilities. These are the given basics with which we all start. Early love can make it easier to ride life's troubles while maintaining self-esteem and feeling confidently loveable. However the historical, political, sociological or religious context into which we are thrown is, for the most part, outside of an individual's control. Love may make the world more bearable, may make an individual's existence more comprehensive in the context of these larger-scale phenomena, but as a reporter commentating on Bosnia said, 'love cannot stop bullets'. We have to live with the knowledge that our love or the love of others is no guarantee of protection.

Nevertheless, love always rises above such limits, flourishing endlessly in our hopes and imagination, a purpose, a meaning, to guide us through. I cannot think of life without love; it seems as important as water to maintaining life. When love disappears to be replaced by arid doctrine of any sort, by obligations, roles, or duties, then the humans involved achieve less than their full potential.

Although rife with contradictions, well-aimed love with realistic goals and aspirations remains the best that most of us can ever hope for. In order to attain this we should not seek outside of ourselves but rather turn the spotlight in. When we understand ourselves and can still love what we understand, then we are ready to beam that love outwards to the lucky recipients. If they too are ready, as if a mirror, they will shine it back to us.